STEINBECK COUNTRY

The sun, poised just below the horizon,
lights up early morning skies
to outline softly the blue ranges
and the long rivers of fog that fill
the valleys between;

rising higher into midmorning, it penetrates
the forest and filters through great
moss-grown oaks . . .

. . . the blue waters of the bay at noon
reflect its passing;

and in the valley the rippling fields
of grain are as golden as the sun itself
sinking toward the western hills.

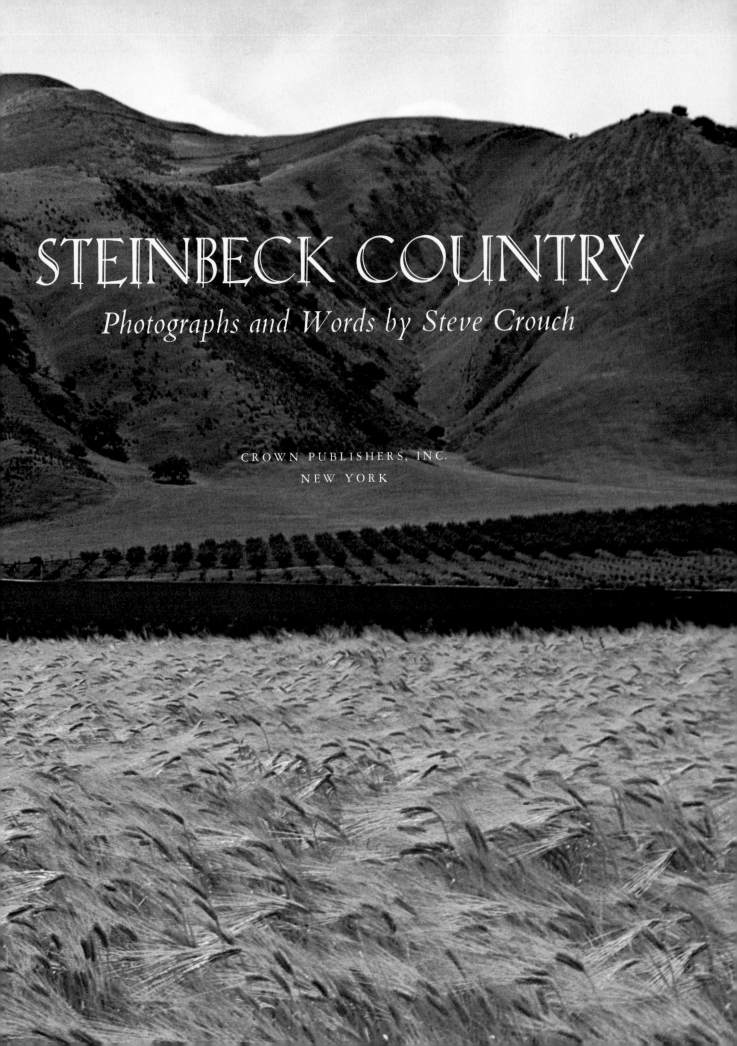

STEINBECK COUNTRY

Photographs and Words by Steve Crouch

CROWN PUBLISHERS, INC.
NEW YORK

For Aaron,
Jon, and Anne Marie

Fifth Printing, August, 1977

Excerpts from the works of John Steinbeck are used here with the permission of the Viking Press, Inc. Page 186 of this book gives full copyright information on these excerpts and is an extension of this copyright page.

Distributed by Crown Publishers, Inc., One Park Avenue, New York, N.Y. 10016.

Library of Congress Card Number 72-95690

ISBN: 0-517-527154
ISBN: 0-517-527162 pbk.

CONTENTS

THE
LAND

THE BEGINNINGS

"First there were Indians, an inferior breed without energy, inventiveness, or culture, a people that lived on grubs and grasshoppers and shellfish, too lazy to hunt or fish. They ate what they could pick up and planted nothing. They pounded bitter acorns for flour. Even their warfare was a weary pantomime.

"Then the hard dry Spaniards came exploring through, greedy and realistic, and their greed was for gold or God. They collected souls as they collected jewels. They gathered mountains and valleys, rivers and whole horizons, the way a man might gain title to building lots. These tough, dried-up men moved restlessly up the coast and down. Some of them stayed on grants as large as principalities, given to them by Spanish kings who had not the faintest idea of the gift. . . .

"Then the Americans came—more greedy because there were more of them. They took the lands, remade the laws to make their titles good. And farmholds spread over the land, first in the valleys and then up the foothill slopes, small wooden houses roofed with redwood shakes, corrals of split poles."

— EAST OF EDEN

Long ago in the dim mists of primordial time, some hundred thousand millennia or more, the land mass of what is now called Monterey County in California lay for the most part beneath the shallow waters of the sea. A few hilly island masses stood above the waters. As time slowly went by, the land was lifted, the sea retreated, the island hills became mountains. Volcanoes were here; the earth shook often as it was folded and crumpled. The land subsided and the sea came in again, until some violent cataclysmic upthrust raised the old hills up into massive mountains and the sea withdrew again for the last time.

The rains of ten million years nibbled at the slopes of the mountains and erosion cut deep canyons and filled the valleys with fine, rich silt.

Along the shore, where long ago mountains were lifted from the depths of the sea, waves wage unending war against the land, the sea the constant victor.

Life struggled out of the waters of the sea and came haltingly upon the land. Over the ages, those strange and curious organisms that were the precursors of the creatures of our time evolved, multiplied and penetrated the long valley and the coastal hills.

Gray lichen and simple mosses slowly spread among the high mountain crags, the very fact of their being there encouraging the process of disintegration of the cold, solid granite. Eventually grasses and shrubs and low trees took hold in those slight crannies and clefts where a little decomposed granite had become soil, slowing the erosion that had already shaped the ranges into the form they have today.

Later, glaciers came down from the Arctic and formed an immense ice barrier across the northern part of the continent. When the Ice Ages drew to a close, the glaciers retreated and a life form new to this hemisphere crossed over the land bridge far to the north, where the old world and the new stand closest together. Slowly, so slowly, they wandered south across the tundra into the endless evergreen forests of the Far North. Over a span of perhaps a thousand years, these ancient men made their way to the central plains and mountains and shores of the American land mass.

Some stayed in the wide grassy plains and became nomadic hunters, following the immense herds of game. Some lived in the eastern hardwood forests, learning to plant seeds in the earth, which they tilled with sharpened, fire-hardened sticks. Others found their final homes on the tops of ancient mesas of the southwestern deserts and in cliff caves and became a fortress people.

Beyond the blazing, endless deserts and west of the highest mountain barriers, along the shores of the great western sea and in its coastal valleys, another wave of these migrants from the north made their way to become shell fishermen in the cold waters and gatherers of acorns from the nearby forests. They drew together in scattered clans—the Essalen, the Costanoan, the Salinan—along these shores and in these upland meadows.

Here they remained, essentially peaceful and undisturbed for ten thousand years or more. They were as much creatures of the land as their mammalian cousins, the grizzly, the gray fox, and the field mouse. Generation succeeded generation and they remained the same, not so much masters of the land as coequals, compromising with it. Civilizations came into being in Sumer, Babylon, and in all the other ancient places of the earth, only to recede into dust and forgotten decay. Troy, Mycenae, Athens, and Rome rose, flourished, and collapsed. Still the people along the shores of California lived out the measured, undisturbed course of their days.

Then, at the end of the Dark Ages, savage Turks swept out of the unknown reaches of Central Asia and overran the lands around the eastern Mediterranean. They seized Constantinople and severed both the water and land trade routes that Venice and the merchant city-states of Italy had established with the Spice Islands, India, and Cathay.

The Europeans, faced by such formidable barriers blocking their way to the East, looked about for new trade routes, and thus it was that they made their way westward beyond the Pillars of Hercules and across the great unknown waters that the ancients had called the Ocean River. They landed at last on these shores, the first small bands but the forerunners of a wave of marauding conquerors, killing, plundering, colonizing along both coasts of the continent. The easily accessible lands in the East were settled first, a century and a half before the Spaniards moved north from Mexico into California to raise their flag and hold the land against the British, French, Russians, and Americans, and all the other rapacious ones who coveted these lands.

The Spaniards, under the aegis of the flag and the cross, corralled the Indians into mission compounds to begin their eternal salvation and, in the process, ensured their obliteration. Within a hundred years of the initial colonization of the shores of Monterey Bay and the nearby valleys, only a handful of Indians were left. Within another century only one lone Indian remained; the rest had disappeared, forgotten and unlamented.

The Spanish and their brothers the Mexicans remained for seventy-five years. Then as the westward trickle across the continent grew into a massive push, the Hispano-Mexicans were pushed aside, ground under, absorbed, dispossessed by a horde of land- and gold-hungry Americans, the final conquerors.

There were further immigrations that added new zest to the mix of Indian, Spanish, Mexican, and Anglo-Saxon peoples. In the long Salinas Valley industrious Italian-Swiss and Danish families bought land and established flourishing enclaves. Near where the Salinas River enters the sea, along the banks of the small River of the Birds, the Pajaro, Croats from the Balkans planted apple orchards. To the coast at the south end of the great crescent bay came Sicilians, Portuguese, Chinese, Japanese, and some of every sort and color of mankind to settle there and lend their own flavor to the place.

Even later, a great wave of the dispossessed, blown out of Oklahoma and Texas and Kansas by constant winds that picked up the soil and sent it east in thick, choking clouds ten thousand feet high, came in and stubbornly sent down roots in cardboard and tin-can shacktowns such as Pajaro, Seaside, and Alisal, even while they were being harassed, beaten, and jailed by police and vigilante groups up and down the length of the state.

So the land was settled, carved up, divided. Where the Indian and the Mexican had lived upon the land and had been tempered by it, the American altered it in a hundred years far more than nature herself had changed it in a hundred thousand.

Among the people who came here were some who told a little of its story—Richard Henry Dana, a Boston boy in the hide trade; Robert Louis Stevenson, following his love across half the world to a small adobe in Monterey; and a host of others—the Comte de la Perouse, Captain George Vancouver, Mary Austin, George Sterling, Jack London, Robinson Jeffers, Lillian Ross.

But the story itself remained in large part untold until the son of a miller in Salinas was born and grew up there, walked the dusty roads between the farms, and listened to the varied tongues of the people of the valley and those along the shores of the bay until he knew perfectly the sound of all their voices and the smells and tastes and feel of this magnificent place. This knowledge lay inside him in ferment until, when he had grown, he began to set it all down on paper.

He told the story of this place as no one had before or probably ever will again. He was at his best when he wrote of this land and its people. What he wrote of them will be enjoyed when most contemporary fiction has entered the twilight realm of the praised unread. Through his words, the world learned of these hills and valleys and waters, and of the people who actually lived there: Doc, La Ida, Lee Chong, Dora Flood, Pilon, Henri the painter, Samuel Hamilton, and a thousand more that he knew. And he told of others who lived only in the byways of his mind until he brought them forth to take their places beside their flesh-and-blood brothers: Mac, Hazel, the Pirate, Lennie and George, Rosasharn, Jesus Maria Corcoran.

There they remain, alive as ever in a procession of pages of eloquent prose—those who lived and those who never were—peopling the lovely land that this spinner of tales so made his own that it will be "Steinbeck Country" as long as the written word persists.

THE MOUNTAINS

" 'What's on the other side?' he asked his father once.

" 'More mountains, I guess. Why?'

" 'And on the other side of them?'

" 'More mountains. Why?'

" 'More mountains on and on?'

" 'Well, no. At last you come to the ocean.'

" 'But what's in the mountains?'

" 'Just cliffs and brush and rocks and dryness.'

" 'Were you ever there?'

" 'No.'

" 'Has anybody ever been there?'

" 'A few people, I guess. It's dangerous, with cliffs and things.
   Why, I've read there's more unexplored country in the mountains
   of Monterey County than any place in the United States.'
   His father seemed proud that this should be so.

" 'And at last the ocean?'

" 'At last the ocean.'

" 'But,' the boy insisted, 'but in between? No one knows?'

" 'Oh, a few people do, I guess. But there's nothing there to get.
   And not much water. Just rocks and cliffs and greasewood. Why?'

" 'It would be good to go.'

" 'What for? There's nothing there.' "

—THE RED PONY

*The serrated mountains rise up, great ridges
that separate the valley from the sea.*

The Santa Lucia Range stretches for more than a hundred miles, from Monterey almost to San Luis Obispo. It is not a single ridge but several ranks of long mountains that parallel the coast. In between is a jumble of transverse ridges and deep canyons. At their highest point they rise to six thousand feet, and at their western edge they plunge directly into the sea.

The whole massive complex is covered with a mantle of scrub intermixed with hardwood and evergreen forest. Ponderosa and sugar pines are native here, as are canyon and valley oaks, redwoods, tanbark oaks, and laurels. Where the tall conifers grow, the slopes and canyons are open and free of underbrush. But for the most part, the mountains are covered with a tangle of scrub oak, hollyleaf cherry, chamise, and a dozen other thicketlike shrubs. Passage is difficult for all but small mammals. Cattle, horses, and men have been lost in these mazes and found years later, bleached bones in some deep gully.

Across the Salinas Valley to the east are the Gabilans, the westernmost mountains of the system known as the Interior Coast Range, which separates the Salinas from the Central Valley. The Gabilans are lesser mountains than the Santa Lucias, lower, less steep, and much drier. Along their eastern edge runs the uneasy scar of the San Andreas Fault, California's major seismic zone. Scattered through the range are many lava plugs and basaltic monoliths, evidence of ancient volcanic origins.

The western slopes of the Gabilans are grass-covered, the heavy scrub and trees restricted to the canyons and the higher ridges. The vegetation resembles that of more arid parts of the state. The predominant conifer here is the digger pine with its sparse, gray-green foliage. On the peaks are small groves of Coulter pine, dark green and massive, their huge cones armed with sharp spines.

On clear mornings the sun hangs for a moment on the rim of the mountain, a brilliant spot ready to light the stage for a new day.

Because the Gabilans are covered most of the year with dried, yellow grasses, they have a warm, welcoming air about them, and the light on their slopes is bright and golden. By contrast, the Santa Lucias, because of their heavier vegetation and some indescribable violet quality of the light, are cool and blue and dark. The outlines of the lower foothills are often lost against the higher ridges beyond, so that, when seen from a distance, the peaks seem to rise straight up from the valley floor. A closer look will reveal that from the canyons opening on the valley great bajadas spread, alluvial fans of detritus washed from the mountainsides by a million years of rainstorms. Judging from the size of these fans, the mountains must have been much higher when they were young, before erosion wore them down.

On the lower slopes bordering the Salinas Valley, cattle and sheep browse in small numbers until the grass gives out in the late summer, but the undergrowth on these mountains makes them unsuitable for large-scale stock raising. That is the specialty of the ranches in the Gabilans, where there is no water for irrigation and no crops can be raised. The grass slopes are covered with cattle from late autumn to midsummer, when the herds are shipped to ranches in Oregon and northern California that have water and grass in abundance.

Inhospitable as they may look to the casual observer, both the Gabilans and the Santa Lucias are full of wildlife. Major predators are scarce; the mountain lion has been reduced to small numbers by professional hunters, and the grizzly bear disappeared seventy years ago. But lesser predators are in both ranges in force—foxes and coyotes, bobcats and weasels, snakes and hawks. Their food supply is abundant—deer, quail, rabbits, and a vast company of mice and gophers.

Only last year, to the surprise of everyone, a brown bear ambled down from the canyons of the Santa Lucias, across the farms on the valley floor, and into the town of Greenfield. It was met with confusion and alarm until it was cornered by rangers from the Fish and Game Department, who roped it and hustled it back into some deep, lost fastness of the mountains. Even the old men who had seen bear in their youth here had thought them extinct in these parts.

Scattered along the slopes of the ridges are small potreros—mountain meadows of a sort—grassy glades surrounded by thicket and forest. By the time midsummer has come, the grasses are burnt dry and the potreros turn to splashes of gold on the blue-green mountainsides.

In the springtime many of these potreros, emerald green after winter rains, come alive with dozens of flowering trees, the legacy of some long-abandoned farmstead that time has leveled with only an occasional chalkrock foundation to mark its passing. The houses are gone, the barns are gone, the fences rotted away, and the people long since departed, leaving their dead behind them in lonely graves guarded by sagging, nameless crosses.

These are the lands where squatters came after the goldfields in the Sierra Nevada played out, settling on the steep slopes and defying landowners on the valley floors to evict them. The hidalgos were often too easygoing to confront these trespassers, and the Americans were too busy pushing out the Mexicans to bother.

But what man could not or would not do, nature did without effort. The people, clinging desperately to these steep slopes, lost what scrawny cattle they had to thickets and canyons, to grizzlies and mountain lions, and to thieves. They lacked water; they lacked almost every necessity that reason demanded they should have to put down roots in such a hostile environment. And so they were beaten by the mountains and drifted away to live in the little towns springing up in the valley

Great gray pines cling to the sparse soil of crannies on the hard volcanic cliffs.

or to end their days working as tenants on some other man's farm.

And in the potreros, no longer disturbed by man, the deer come up at twilight from their hiding places and move gently and effortlessly up the slopes and along the skyline, their semaphored ears wagging at the sound of the wind or the scolding of a squirrel or the snapping of a twig under a hoof. The red-tailed hawk, his spread feathers molten copper in the declining sun, makes great circles as he rides the updrafts from the heated hills, his head turning from side to side to search for ground squirrels or field mice on the earth below.

These are the peaceful meadows of the sky, shining golden pendants upon the dark breast of this splendid range of hills.

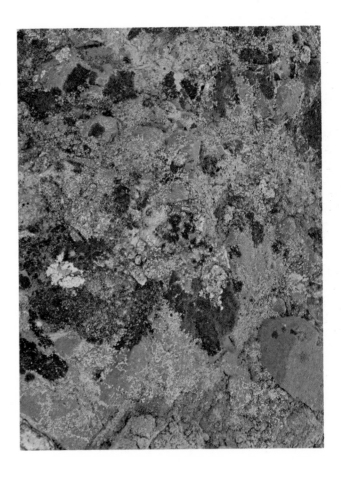

In these dry mountains the xerophilic chamise covers the slopes, while the red cliffs wear a Jacob's coat of brilliant lichens.

The sun took a long time to set on the last day of May. From the top of the highest ridge on Buck Wiley's ranch—the old Rancho Arroyo Seco, where the Sierra de Salinas ends by plunging steeply into the canyon of the Arroyo Seco—the Santa Lucia range to the west was rim-lit interminably by the hot glare of the sun hanging poised above the Pacific; meanwhile across the valley the highest peak of the Gabilans and the jagged volcanic plugs of the Pinnacles were turning a deep red. The valley itself was already preparing for the night, drawing a pale lavender veil over itself, while the lights of Soledad and King City went on and grew brighter as the shadow cast by the Santa Lucias crept up the face of the eastern hills.

In the meadows where close-sheared sheep nibbled at the dry, short grass, deer came out of the chaparral to browse, their new antlers in full velvet. A badger that, since the Christmas before, had been methodically working his way through the long-established ground squirrel colony above the water tank, poked his striped head from the hole beneath the huge boulder on the far slope and stood immobile on his doorstep for a long time, testing the wind. At length, satisfied, he stepped forth and ambled off toward the squirrel burrows in search of his evening meal.

Only Junipero Serra peak, the highest of the Santa Lucias, was still touched by the sun. Then, in a final orange flush, the sun was gone and the light faded to magenta, to lavender, to the blue-gray of twilight.

Far off to the north, from the direction of Gonzales, the faint bellow of a diesel floated on the wind, and the flashing Mars light on the lead engine of a long train of refrigerator cars came into sight, heading toward King City and Los Angeles.

Suddenly, from somewhere beyond one of the western ridges, a golden eagle came rocketing over the crest and, wings held rigid for maximum glide, shot down the east slope and disappeared into the dusk of a canyon far below.

Before the light had faded in the west, the moon rose over the mountains beyond Bitterwater Valley in the Gabilans. While the sun had seemingly lingered on and on before slipping into night, the moon came up quickly, blood red in the haze and smoke that floats down from Moss Landing and San Jose to fill the valley on such hot days.

The smooth red bark of the madrone tree splits and peels away—an outgrown garment cast off each year.

And so the procession of the heavens went: Venus, brightest in the twilight sky, following the sun down behind Chews Ridge, while Jupiter and Saturn hung high in the sky above, fully visible even before the first stars faintly appeared. Later the red point of light that was Mars followed the moon out of the east.

The noises of the day began to fade. All day the low mutter of diesel trucks on the freeway in the valley had reached the high ridges, but with dark the sounds no longer came. The trucks were there, but only their headlights betrayed them, marking the long ribbon of road from where it came into sight just south of Chualar and made its way across miles of flat fields to where it disappeared south of King City behind the low hills that close in on the narrowing valley.

The grasses, parched by the early drought, whispered in the suddenly cool breeze that came sweeping in from the distant ocean. Somewhere, unexpectedly on this dry slope, a small frog chirped, and a chorus of his kind replied.

As the moon rose higher, entering the second quadrant of the heavens, it softly illuminated the ridges to the south that were now black masses outlined against higher black masses. The haze flowed into the canyons between the ranges like little rivers, and the mountains and valleys had the look of a Chinese brush-and-ink drawing—amorphous, unreal, more beautiful by suggestion than in reality.

South across the canyon of the Arroyo Seco shone the lights of the ranch house at the head of Reliz Road, the only light in the entire Santa Lucia Range. Yet east across the valley, the headlights of cars coming across the Gloria grade and those winding down the Pinnacles road winked in and out as they inched down to the valley floor. Lights on the Bitterwater Road on the crest east of King City flared up momentarily; and faintly, fifty miles or more to the southeast, the lonely lights of a car on the Mustang grade stabbed the night and then disappeared.

The breeze, growing colder as the night advanced, subsided, and the faint sounds of the mountain became audible—the rustle of a deer mouse scuttling through the dry grass in search of seeds; the snarling of raccoons arguing on the slopes below; the faint yapping of a coyote ranging the crest of a far ridge. Floating through the night, the pungent aroma of a striped skunk announced his passing.

Over the years the night has been peopled by other presences that have passed this way before: Gaspar de Portolá's exhausted band, which climbed wearily across the Santa Lucias two hundred years ago on the way to rediscover the Bay of Monterey; Old Gabriel, who was a young man when Padre Serra converted him and who outlasted all his Indian peers and white masters to die, full of years and wisdom, at the age of 151; Tiburcio Vásquez, who galloped up the steep slopes and into the sheltering brush, safe from pursuing posses; Samuel Hamilton, gallant Irishman of shining spirit, who struggled for existence in the hardscrabble hills east of King City and who was immortalized by a tale-teller of a grandson named Steinbeck; and old Alberto Trescony, that honest and industrious tinsmith from northern Italy, whose only advice to his sons was, "Buy Land," and who sleeps forever on the little eminence south of San Lucas, above the lands he loved so well, Rancho San Benito and Rancho San Lucas.

In this valley and in these mountains, the men who came from Europe to claim the land for distant sovereigns and who remained to claim it for themselves, as well as those who took it from them later, still make their presence felt—in the names and legends they left behind them and in the sons who followed them.

By midsummer the potreros are bright splashes of color on the mountainsides; deer graze these slopes, their semaphored ears wagging at sounds on the wind.

STEINBECK COUNTRY:
A PORTFOLIO

*Storms of the autumn equinox send heavy clouds
pressing in against the Santa Lucias.*

Man's back roads in the Gabilans are white scars on the chalky soil; on the bajadas of the Santa Lucias, the roads of erosion leave deep gashes in hillside pastures.

In the dusty, bone-dry valleys of the Gabilans, oats and barley are
the only crops the waterless land will support.

Plastic sheets covering strawberry fields catch the rays of the afternoon sun—a great reflecting mirror set in the middle of black fields.

Utility roads cut precise paths through the ordered fields of the valley, but in the hills the roads meander around ranches and over ridges almost aimlessly.

Great white billows coast along the crest of the Gabilans, but on the
high, sea-facing slopes of the Sur, dark clouds, heavy with rain, draw a
veil across the sun.

Far offshore the storms of winter build up huge waves and send them surging landward to spend themselves in thunder against the rocky cliffs.

43

THE PASTURES OF HEAVEN

"In the late afternoon of the second day a small deer started up before the troop and popped out of sight over a ridge. The corporal disengaged himself from his column and rode in its pursuit. His heavy horse scrambled and floundered up the steep slope; the manzanita reached sharp claws for the corporal's face, but he plunged on after his dinner. In a few minutes he arrived at the top of the ridge, and there he stopped, stricken with wonder at what he saw—a long valley floored with green pasturage on which a herd of deer browsed. Perfect live oaks grew in the meadow of the lovely place, and the hills hugged it jealously against the fog and the wind.

"The disciplinarian corporal felt weak in the face of so serene a beauty. He who had whipped brown backs to tatters, he whose rapacious manhood was building a new race for California, this bearded, savage bearer of civilization slipped from his saddle and took off his steel hat.

"'Holy Mother!' he whispered. 'Here are the green pastures of Heaven to which our Lord leadeth us.'"

—THE PASTURES OF HEAVEN

Beyond the gentle Corral de Tierra, the northern ridges of the Santa Lucias slope down to meet the sea.

If you hold out your hand, cup it lightly, and then tilt it so it slants toward you, it will resemble nothing so much as the great, wrinkled earthen bowl that the Spaniards called the "Corral de Tierra" and John Steinbeck called the "Pastures of Heaven."

On three sides it is ringed by the high ridges of the Sierra de Salinas and the lesser mountains of the northern Santa Lucia range. On the fourth side, it opens into the winding flood plain of Toro Creek that flows down toward the Salinas Valley.

It has a pleasant country road that makes a great circle up and around the long meadows on the lower slopes of Mount Toro. Then it climbs sharply up over a ridge and drops gently down into the San Benancio Canyon and back to the Salinas highway. On the way it goes past an eroded sandstone cliff formation that stands high above the valley. The people in the Corral de Tierra call it "The Castle." The British explorer, George Vancouver, saw it from a distance two hundred years ago and thought the cliffs a Spanish fortress, forbidding and impregnable.

The valley used to be a place of white-faced cattle and black-tailed deer, of scuttling plumed quail and circling hawks. In its higher reaches it still is, but lower down it is a place of golf courses and subdivisions. Even so, enough of its peaceful beauty remains that it is clear what caused Steinbeck's corporal to cry out in wonder at the sight below him.

In winter, when heavy clouds from the Pacific bring cold rains, the small streams of the Corral de Tierra run bank-full, and the snow lies lightly on the top and flanks of Mount Toro. When the days begin to lengthen, the first to react are the willows along the watercourses, putting forth small velvet catkins along their bare branches. Spring is heralded by the blue blossoms of half a dozen kinds of lupine and the orange California poppies that spring up on the open slopes, blazes of color that are the particular splendor of California. The valley is a soft green, and the air is filled with the small sounds of birds pausing on the long journey northward.

Of all the valleys of Monterey County, none is more tranquil and lovely than the upper slopes of this meadowland, ringed about by hills that cut it off as effectively from the main centers of population as they did when the Spanish governor granted it to Guadalupe Figueroa. Twenty years later all of the Hispano-Mexicans had been elbowed out—not a scrap of land remained in the hands of the original owners. All of it had been presented by the United States Land Commission to American claimants who were clamoring loudly for land and more land.

During the years that followed, the lower end of the valley near the Monterey-Salinas highway fell into the possession of Swiss-Italians; their descendants are still numerous there today. In the upper end the larger parcels are still practically intact, lands once part of the extensive holdings of David Jacks, one of California's great land barons.

Here and there beside the newcomers are families who have been in this valley for a century or more. The Diaz brothers live at the upper end of Corral de Tierra where the road climbs over the

Old wood barns, scoured by the rains of fifty winters and dried by the hot summer sun, grow as ridged and furrowed as the land about them.

ridge into San Benancio Canyon. They live on land their grandfather claimed 119 years ago, when he tired of his life as a whaler and turned to following cattle instead of whales. His grandson, old Ben Diaz, lives in his house under the live oak trees at the base of the hills, his dooryard filled with grapevines taken a hundred years ago from the abandoned mission in Carmel and set out here in the warm sunshine. Now, when autumn frosts brush them, they turn brilliant yellow and scarlet, the brightest splash of color in all the valley.

Lower down, where the oaks make a park near the old Washington School, lies the land that Eusebio Molera, son-in-law of Juan Bautista Rogers Cooper, bought from David Jacks. The land passed in the course of years into the steward-ship of his son. Andrew Molera was a huge man, standing six feet one in his handmade cowboy boots; with his white Stetson on, he measured almost seven feet from toe to crown.

He was a man of enormous appetite. He thought nothing of eating a whole turkey at one sitting or a clutch of steaks, garnished with potatoes and gravy, and with a cluster of side dishes—all washed down with the *vin du pays*. He weighed in at something more than four hundred pounds. When he drove over from Monterey in his chain-driven Mercedes to see after his property, the automobile roared up the dirt road in a billow of white dust, listing far to the left under his weight.

There are those of sharp memory who recall watching with awe, when they were children, as he sat at table and ate his way through course after course. One lady of mature years can remem-ber a summer day more than half a century ago when her father encountered Molera along the

road that ran between their lands and invited him to lunch. Molera accepted with alacrity, and the rancher arrived home with his guest in tow to confront a furious wife. Unexpected guests were frequent and usually posed no special problems; but this was no ordinary guest, and his reputation had preceded him. The lady of the house took her husband aside and remonstrated with him, pointing out that the larder, while not empty, was inadequate for an event of this magnitude.

However, the tradition of hospitality in those days being what it was, by hurriedly improvising and mixing and stewing and whatever arcane things women do in such situations, a meal of double or triple the usual size was set in due course before the visitor. The children had been taken aside privately and warned to eat little lest there not be enough for the guest of honor. But what child could do more than dabble at food when his eyes were wide with wonder at the disappearance with unbelievable dispatch of all the food upon the table, food which under normal circumstances would have fed the household for a full day or even more?

At length Molera, full of thanks and belches, took his leave, after assuring his hostess that the meal would be sufficient until he could get back to Monterey to his own more substantial table. Then, with his appetite at least momentarily assuaged, he stepped into his automobile with the permanent cant to port and chuffed off down the road to disappear into heat waves in the distance, leaving behind him a marveling pair of small children to watch his departure through gaps in the white picket fence.

Such were the tales told of this latter-day Anglo-Hispanic hidalgo. He lived a full, rich life, replete with honors and accomplishments. He became a legend in his own time and was cut off by a gastric disturbance in his prime.

The Corral de Tierra and its neighboring canyon, the San Benancio, are more closely allied with Salinas than with Monterey, because of the proximity and similarity of outlook. But sometimes people of the Peninsula, tired of fog, move to Corral de Tierra. And a sizable number from the flatlands of Salinas, most of whom secretly look upon themselves as true descendants of the Old West, move up into these hills and establish their one-acre spreads. The valley is full of corrals and horses. The people affect cowboy boots, faded Levis, and properly dented white Stetsons with precisely rolled brims. Along the lower stretches of San Benancio Canyon, the number of cars in the driveways is exceeded only by the number of horses in the corrals.

In the higher reaches and on the slopes of Toro, the ranches are still there. How long they will be there is anybody's guess; but when taxes mount so high that the ranchers can no longer afford to keep them, the tracts will edge up the slopes, and where once the rare white quail lived, the land will become suburbia.

In the protected meadows tiny baby blue-eyes grow, sheltered from the cold winds and fog that course along the ridges far above.

*There is a very special quality to spring in the
Pastures of Heaven, a velvet softness of the land that
defies description.*

*An old schoolhouse, once noisy with the voices
of generations long gone, slowly crumbles back into
the soil.*

THE RIVER VALLEY

"The Salinas was only a part-time river. The summer sun drove it underground. It was not a fine river at all, but it was the only one we had so we boasted about it—how dangerous it was in a wet winter and how dry it was in a dry summer. You can boast about anything if it's all you have. Maybe the less you have, the more you are required to boast."

—EAST OF EDEN

Among the rivers of the world, the Salinas is a minor one indeed, perhaps not much more than a hundred fifty miles in length. It rises in the hills between San Luis Obispo and Paso Robles, when the cold winter rains beat upon the ridges and the secret porous reservoirs deep within the mountains, filled to overflowing, burst forth in seeps and springs that start the waters on their way north toward the distant sea.

It runs brimful to the limits of its banks as long as the rains come down. It roars past San Miguel, where Camp Roberts sits astride its course. Here it enters Monterey County, twisting through a flood plain that it has cut during the course of a million years through the ridges and upthrusts. Past Bradley and San Ardo it goes, past the bobbing pumps of the wells of Texaco and Shell and Getty that lift a thin flow of black oil from the depths of the earth.

More gently now, as the gradient of the valley lessens, it slides past the point where the great ranches of San Bernardo, San Benito, and San Lucas come together. At King City and Greenfield it goes between sandy dunes where the wind in summer whips gray sand around the dry brush that grows there.

North of Greenfield, near where the river curls west around Soledad, is its confluence with the Arroyo Seco which means in English, "dry gulch." For most of the year the Arroyo Seco fits its name. But when the winter rains begin, it becomes the roaring outlet for all water in the northern Santa Lucias east of the main north-south ridge. As the water pours down every slope and canyon, it cascades over a hundred foaming crests in this mountain basin and into the only stream that drains it—the Arroyo Seco. Then the Arroyo Seco roars out through a gap in the hills onto the flat plain of the Salinas. Sometimes when the burden of water is greater than the stream can carry, it bursts its banks and becomes a mile-wide lake where its waters join those of the Salinas.

The farmers who live here watch winter storms uneasily; when the word comes that the Arroyo Seco is on the rampage, livestock are rounded up and driven out, and families move to higher ground. The waters rise as one storm follows another until the Arroyo Seco spreads out into a watery wasteland with only a few cows, abandoned in the general exodus, left bawling atop the scattered islands in the flood's path.

Below Soledad, the channel of the Salinas is

For more than a hundred miles, the Salinas flows through the fertile valley it has carved.

53

wide enough to hold between its banks all the floodwaters of the upper Salinas and the Arroyo Seco. It flows on, turgid with brown silt from the mountains, past Gonzales and Chualar to the weathered old sugar refinery that Claus Spreckels built a century ago at the foot of Mount Toro, just south of Salinas. At this point the river sometimes leaves its banks again and floods all the low lettuce and artichoke fields that lie between here and the ocean.

At last the river reaches the sea and empties into the surf, its burden of mud and silt making a great brown fan in the blue waters of the bay. Indeed, such has been its force in ages past that in the floor of the bay and extending well into the ocean floor beyond lies a canyon cut by the river that reaches a depth of 12,000 feet below the waves.

The rains of April give way to the drying winds of late spring and summer, but for a month after the rainy season ends, the river runs full into the sea. Gradually the small brooks and springs begin to dry up. At the same time, the farmers begin heavy irrigation of their fields so that, in due course, more of the river is pumped upon the fields than flows into the ocean. Then the mouth silts over and the waves build great sandbars to dam the river from the sea. The Salinas in its final reaches below Spreckels becomes a mere trickle by the middle of summer, abloom with algae, choked with reeds, and reeking of decay. The Arroyo Seco, tapped near its end for water for the grapes of the Wente Brothers, goes completely dry. Its last miles before reaching the Salinas become a dusty, sandy track, host to the roaring Yamahas and Kawasakis of the young men from the nearby ranches and farms, mechanized descendants of the vaqueros of two centuries ago.

Since men first came into this valley, the Salinas, never a picturesque watercourse, has had one overriding virtue: without its existence men would not be here. For the Salinas, with its few tributaries—the San Antonio, the Arroyo Seco, the Nacimiento

—is the only source of water for a hundred and fifty miles, and it has been harnessed and used with an almost unbelievable efficiency.

Dams have been thrown across the San Antonio and Nacimiento rivers in the Santa Lucias. When winter rains come, the lakes behind the dams fill to overflowing. In summer, when the Salinas begins to subside and sink into its sands, the spillways are opened and a carefully controlled torrent is loosed into the Salinas.

So it is that the Salinas is a free-flowing river the year around, from Bradley in the south, through San Ardo, King City, Soledad, and Gonzales, to Chualar. Then suddenly, between Chualar and Salinas, the river stops running and stands in stagnant pools. For a hundred miles the farmers have pumped its waters onto their fields until its current is stilled near its end—not enough water remains to flow the last ten miles to the sea.

Through the years, the Salinas has been a river of more parts than meet the eye; beneath its sands and stretching from the Santa Lucias on the west to the Gabilans on the east is an underground river of enormous proportions. The farmers on the lands here have sunk a thousand or more wells to tap this supply for their fields.

The Salinas River is literally mined for its water. There have been times when the drain on the water supply to irrigate fields and water lawns and golf courses has been so heavy that the underground water has been depleted; then waters from the sea have percolated in to pollute the water table near Castroville, and artichoke fields there have been endangered by the brackish water.

As long as the rains fall in winter and the lakes behind the dam are full, the river will water the valley and sustain its people. But if the rains should fail, as they have done at times in the past, the lakes and the river would dry up and the fields would turn sere and desolate. Then drought would grip the valley and the great green cornucopia would be empty.

The fields—cultivated, fertilized, and
pampered by the men who tend them—
respond with great abundance.

In summer, when water is poured upon the land
with prodigality, mist from the sprinklers catches the
afternoon sun in a thousand little rainbows to
delight the eye.

But where the river, robbed of its living water,
stands quiet and still near the sea, algae and other
water plants form a green blanket on its surface.

Twilight along the river brings a hush broken only by the whisper
of water and the cheerful sounds of an unseen host of frogs.

"And then—remember?—the train whistle and the boring light and a freight train from King City would go stomping across Castroville Street and into Salinas and you could hear it sighing at the station. Remember?"

—East of Eden

There is a long string of towns along the Salinas River from its source to the sea. After it comes down out of the San Rafael range, it flows past Atascadero, Paso Robles, and San Miguel in San Luis Obispo County. It enters Monterey County just south of Bradley, now a dying crossroads since the freeway bypassed it. The freeway, designed by men whose duty it is to move traffic around such little towns, also took away the strong pulse of commerce from the next two towns to the north, San Ardo and San Lucas, and left them drowsing in the sun. San Ardo will hold out for a while because of the nearby oil fields, but San Lucas and Bradley will probably disappear.

The towns farther north—King City, Greenfield, Soledad, Gonzales, and Salinas—are of a different stripe. They sit in the middle of some of the most fertile land on earth. They serve as mercantile centers, bedroom communities for the men who work in the fields, and shipping points on the Southern Pacific for the produce from these fields.

The towns are where they are because a century ago they marked successive railheads as the Southern Pacific slowly laid its tracks southward from San Francisco toward Los Angeles. Each time the tracks were extended, a community sprang up around the temporary terminus. The towns were given a solid base for their economies, a base that lasts to this day.

These are in effect company towns, all tied to an agrarian economy of enormous proportions. Their primary concerns are unlimited water, cheap labor, and a favorable agricultural market. Given a sufficiency of these requisites, the farms gross a rich money harvest, and the benefits are diffused through all the towns of the valley.

Residents of the towns along the river are primarily of two ethnic stocks, Nordic and Latin. The Anglo-Saxons and the Italians hold the reins for the most part; the Hispano-Mexicans, who call themselves Chicanos, are not within the power structure. Added to these peoples are a sprinkling of prosperous Basques in the southern towns, and in Salinas, at the other end of the valley, a considerable number of Orientals, Filipinos, and an increasing number of blacks.

The prosperous middle-class burghers who live in the tract-house subdivisions of the valley towns all appear to have been cast in the same mold.

Their aims, their interests, and their pastimes are the same, and the rare deviant is looked upon as little short of subversive. These people constitute the bulwark of conservative movements—political, economic, and religious. They secretly suspect most people of the Monterey Peninsula and the Big Sur of being somewhat radical and not really to be trusted.

In common with agricultural towns of all the California valleys, those from Salinas to King City have a subculture—*in* the towns but not really *of* them—a subculture of bums and drunks who live in doorways and hallways and flophouses, and provide a life's work for caseworkers of the county welfare department. They subsist on bad whiskey, muscatel, and the other fortified wines plentiful along whatever skid row they inhabit at the moment. They are of all races save the Oriental. Some are native; some came in the successive waves of migration from the states to the east. They exist in a permanent state of bibulous euphoria or drunken anesthesia (depending upon one's point of view) as long as the wine is available, and they sink to horrible depths when it is not. They dry out periodically in the county jail or county hospital, a sort of involuntary retrenchment before sliding back into the old alcoholic haze.

Since they are unemployable and not welcome in the fields, they drift about the streets of Salinas and the other towns, a fraternity of the lost. Across the railroad tracks in Salinas, close by the district where the Chinese still live and where fan-tan joints and whorehouses once flourished, they float from one sleazy bar to another while there is money to spend on whiskey, and they retire to weed-grown vacant lots with their muscatel when money is in short supply. This proximity to the railroad right-of-way sometimes leads one of them to stumble along the tracks until he falls senseless, to be ground under a fast-moving freight pulling out of the yards onto the main line, his only epitaph a short paragraph in the *Salinas Californian*.

But for the most part, protected by some whimsical providence that seems to guard their kind, the winos move around the fringes of the respectable people, as disdainful as they are disdained, on an almost permanent plateau of induced joie de vivre. For instance, one early foggy morning not long ago one well-oiled derelict, moved by some inner compulsion to go from Here to There, arose and stumbled across the tracks and out upon Main Street in Salinas. The streets were full of cars and pedestrians en route to work, the walkers avoiding each other on the sidewalks, the cars feinting and charging each other on the streets. The drunk moved in measured, solemn, erratic steps along the sidewalk, caroming off buildings and pedestrians with equal aplomb. At length he reached an intersection where the lights flipped from green to yellow to red and back again, and the people and cars charged and stopped and charged again. The drunk screwed up his eyes in an attempt to assess the situation. Failing this, he drew himself erect, with slow deliberation crossed himself, and launched himself directly into the path of traffic. Brakes and watchers screamed, cars skidded, people on the curb held their breath in anticipation of the impending collision between flesh and metal. Through some miracle, he was missed. He stumbled over the curb and up onto the sidewalk, propelled by fervent and awesome oaths hurled after him by the shaken drivers. Unsteadily triumphant, he turned upon his adversaries and, with the most obscene of gestures, bestowed his blessing upon them, then made off unsteadily toward Who Knows Where.

THE PENINSULA

"*In my flurry of nostalgic spite, I have done the Monterey Peninsula a disservice. It is a beautiful place, clean, well run, and progressive. The beaches are clean where once they festered with fish guts and flies. The canneries which once put up a sickening stench are gone, their place filled with restaurants, antique shops, and the like. They fish for tourists now, not pilchards, and that species they are not likely to wipe out. And Carmel, begun by starveling writers and unwanted painters, is now a community of the well-to-do and the retired. If Carmel's founders should return, they could not afford to live there, but it wouldn't go that far. They would be instantly picked up as suspicious characters and deported over the city line.*

"*The place of my origin had changed, and having gone away I had not changed with it. In my memory it stood as it once did and its outward appearance confused and angered me.*"

— TRAVELS WITH CHARLEY

Cypress trees that have withstood the worst that wind and sea can send against them cling to the rocky cliffs—bent, contorted, defiant.

Along the shore, the omnipresent gulls dominate by sheer weight of numbers; every rocky pinnacle is a perch and a lookout. At sunset, they gather in the calm waters to gossip.

Where the rocks of Lobos thrust into the sea, the receding tide exposes teeming pools in every cleft; just beyond the breakers, sea otters play in the kelp beds.

*At low tide starfish cling
immobile in the exposed cracks
and crannies of the cliffs, and
clusters of mussels close tightly
to await the sea's return.*

*When the waters recede, small marine gardens
move gently in the quiet eddies of the ebb tide.*

The colors of the sea are many, subdued in these small starfish, brilliant in the inner surface of an abalone shell scoured by waves and sand.

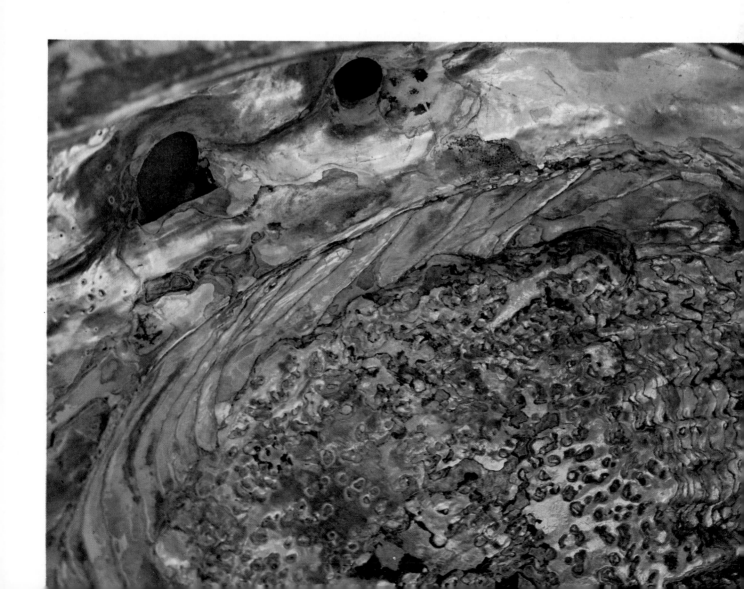

At twilight the great crescent of the bay is marked by the lights of towns along its shore.

71

Glorious are those days when the declining sun sets the skies on fire and the sands below reflect its brilliance.

When the granite spines of the hills of the Monterey Peninsula were first formed, they were cold and barren. As the wind and water of the ages wore away at the rock, pockets of soil accumulated in the crevices of the peaks and in the low places. Then pine seeds, carried to these hills and sea cliffs in the craw of some wandering jay or migrating grosbeak, were left behind, undigested, on receptive soil and sprang to life.

The first trees looked exactly like their parents to the east and north. But in the strange and marvelous way in which nature alters all her living things to create a great diversity, the succeeding generations of pine trees began to change slowly as they responded to the unique qualities of the soil and the prevailing climatic conditions.

In time they became different and distinct from all other pines. Their needles grew in groups of three instead of two or five, their cones were egg-shaped with a whorl at the base, their bark was deeply fissured and dark. They grew fast and tall; they aged quickly and grew old gracefully. They died and slowly crumbled back into the earth.

When they grew close together, their spindly trunks reached high toward the sky, all their branches and greenery thinly clustered at the top so that they resembled nothing so much as a grove of tall, swaying palms with bunched crowns and long, naked trunks. When a strong breeze blew there was the sound of creaking wood, as if a forest of ships' masts were groaning under the impact of wind in their sails.

But when such a pine stood apart, its growth was slower and less abruptly vertical. It had symmetry and stature and dignity, with a massiveness few other pines could match. The top was rounded; the limbs, thickly needled, were spaced equally apart along the trunk. It became a grandfather of a tree, a hundred feet or more in height and as thick at the base as a man is high.

Animals and birds sought the shelter of these trees. Squirrels hurled themselves through the branches and tore the cones apart for their seeds; mice tunneled at the roots. Nuthatches ran up and down the trunks, searching for borers and beetles. The wind sighed through the crowns and bent the highest branches. Yet a great calm was in these forests. Sounds were blunted, and Spanish moss grew long, hanging beards from the lower limbs.

But when these trees grew on the sea cliffs, the constant winds from the ocean battered them unceasingly, bending them toward the land, twisting their branches, and forcing them close to the ground so that they grew dwarfed and stunted. All over the headlands of the Monterey Peninsula and the spiny ridges of Point Lobos, the pines grew thickly, so closely allied to the sea winds and the fog that they never grew more than a few miles from the sea's edge. And they grew in only two other places in the world: on a cliff at the north end of the crescent of Monterey Bay and in a grove a hundred miles south, where the Santa Lucia range dwindles to low hills.

When the land's first men wandered down from the north, they found the forest inviting and the seashore bountiful. Here they remained. Sometimes in the forests, but more often in the great barrens near the sea, they left their multistoried middens—layer upon layer of charred firewood, abalone shell, human bones, and the other accumulated detritus of ten thousand years of communal living. At the mouth of the creek called San Jose near Point Lobos, standing halfway between the sea and the quiet pine forest on the mountain slope, is a great mound sixty feet high. The top twenty feet, probed by curious men who are driven to examine such things, holds a record of more than twenty-five centuries of human habitation. Here, where the sea provided provenance for the tribe, they lived out their generations, retiring to the depths of the nearby pine forest when danger threatened. Atop the bluffs

by the sea are small hollows ground into the living rock, *metates* used by the women of the tribe to grind acorns into flour.

The forest was little affected by the Indians since they had no designs on the land and felt no urge to alter it. The pines grew thick and verdant, and the hills were covered, their spread halted only by an occasional fire set by lightning or tribesmen. The forest, cleared by flames, grew back quickly.

The first white men on these shores noted the tall, straight trees, calculated that they would make good ships' masts, and so reported to the viceroys of Spain in Mexico. But the trees were spared this fate, for the Spanish were content to do no more than establish a small garrison here. It became a seaport much later and was never a refitting point for the galleons sailing past from Manila.

A century and a half later, when the Anglo-Saxons came to explore, to search for riches, and to elbow aside the native Californios, they brought their zoologists and botanists, classifiers who searched the shores and hills, and found a wealth of new plants and trees that existed nowhere else on earth. They found the pine growing in profusion and gave it a Latin name, *Pinus radiata*, but the people called it simply Monterey pine. By that name it has become known throughout the world. With its neighbor, the Monterey cypress, it has been transplanted far and wide as a reforester of wasted slopes, for it grows faster than any other pine. Halfway around the world, in New Zealand, the Monterey pine has become the commercial lumber tree of the Antipodes and stands of it form vast tree farms there.

Long-timers on the Monterey Peninsula tell of how Carmel, across the hill, became a town of trees. When its two original developers, Powers and Devendorf, looked about their newly acquired land shortly after the turn of this century, they found that, except on the uppermost heights, they owned a long slope, stretching away brush-covered and treeless to the ocean on the west and to the ruined mission on the south. They prudently sought the advice of David Jacks, a man of Monterey who had become one of the most successful land barons California ever knew and who had cornered most of the lands around Monterey. Jacks, being wise in the ways of avoiding taxes, suggested that they declare their land a tree farm to seek the lowest possible tax rate.

This they did. Borrowing a horse and wagon and a Chinese man from David Jacks, they went about setting out at random small Monterey pines, which grew in time to form an urban forest, stretching majestic branches over some of the most overinflated real estate in America.

The pines still thrive throughout the Monterey Peninsula, despite the constant onslaughts of new arrivals from Nebraska and Kansas and Southern California who, together with a not inconsiderable number of the native-born, lay diligently about with chain saw and bulldozer in an earnest attempt to convert the land into small replicas of Nebraska or Kansas or Southern California.

But on steep slopes and in gullies too rugged to attract land speculators and subdividers, the trees grow unmolested. At their feet the wild lilacs and native iris, the salal and manzanita grow thick, and small animals hide from their enemies. Deer move in and out of the trees to graze on golf courses that have proliferated where the long-vanished grizzly used to forage. The raccoons come out at dusk in masked battalions to prospect in the dooryards of the nearest houses, while in the soft dark beyond gray foxes slip silently by and disappear like smoke.

Some day, perhaps, when the last man has gone, vanished like the dinosaurs because he, too, could not come to terms with his environment, the trees will still flourish, spreading and covering the wounds man has inflicted upon the land.

Fog draws a blue-gray veil among the trees, and suddenly the forest becomes a cathedral full of soft, pervasive light.

When winter rains fall, boulders and trees in the canyons are covered over with lush green moss, and the air is heavy with the smell of decay.

THE BIG SUR

*"It was a well-worn path, dark soft leaf-mould earth strewn
with broken pieces of sandstone. The trail rounded the shoulder of
the canyon and dropped steeply into the bed of the stream. In the
shallows the water ran smoothly, glinting in the first morning sun.
Small round stones on the bottom were as brown as rust with sun
moss. In the sand along the edges of the stream the tall, rich wild
mint grew, while in the water itself the cress, old and tough, had
gone to heavy seed. . . .*

*"Soon the canyon sides became steep and the first giant
sentinel redwoods guarded the trail, great round red trunks bearing
foliage as green and lacy as ferns. Once Pepé was among the trees,
the sun was lost. A perfumed and purple light lay in the pale
green of the underbrush. Gooseberry bushes and blackberries and
tall ferns lined the stream, and overhead the branches of the
redwoods met and cut off the sky."*

—FLIGHT

The region known as the Big Sur lies south of Monterey, stretching along the coast for eighty miles—eighty miles of canyon, precipice, rocky peak, and redwood forest.

This is not gentle country with easy contours. The Sur is a land of steep ups and downs; there is little level ground. One either climbs laboriously or descends rapidly. The mountains rise out of the Pacific almost at a right angle and keep going up steeply all the way to the tops of the coastal ridges. Along the summits the slopes level out and curve over gently before plunging down again on the reverse side. Drivers rushing along the twisting road on the cliffs above the sea must crane their necks mightily to get an occasional glimpse of the mountaintops above. More than one rusting hulk lies at the water's edge at the base of the cliffs in testimony to the danger of such an endeavor.

The Sur is a place apart—ninety miles of precipitous sea cliffs, soaring mountains, and dark forests.

When the governors of Alta California offered land grants to the soldiers of the Monterey Presidio a century and a half ago, only two grants were requested in the whole coastal reach, the ranchos El Sur and San Jose y Sur Chiquito. Both names referred to streams cutting through the ridges to the sea, from the Creek of St. Joseph in the north to the two rivers of the south which the Spaniards had named El Rio Grande del Sur and El Rio Chiquito del Sur—shortened to Sur Grande and Sur Chiquito. They came into English in literal translation as Big Sur and Little Sur.

Probably the first who lived in these mountains other than Indians were two men who pulled out of Monterey when they found themselves being crowded by Americans. Vicente Avila and Manuel Boronda moved their families and possessions far below Rancho El Sur, down where Cone Peak stands a mile above the Pacific. They filed their claims on the land, and no Americans came near them for twenty years.

Later the first American settlers came and staked their claims on mountain lands north of the ranches of Boronda and Avila. They built their

Where the rivers reach the sea, shifting sandbars block the way and force the streams to shift their courses to find a passage; on the wide, empty beaches only the seabirds are there to watch the passing of the day.

homes in grassy potreros high above the sea—the Danis, Harlans, Posts, Pfeiffers, Partingtons, and two bachelors, Dolan and Anderson. Descendants of these pioneers still live here, and the family names have been attached to the landmarks of this most magnificent of the western highlands—Partington Ridge, Dani Point, Pfeiffer Creek, Post Summit, Vicente Creek, Anderson Canyon, Dolan Creek.

These early settlers lived in relative isolation for more than half a century. The easy road from Monterey stopped just south of where Carmel is now and the rough wagon track into the hills called for a two-day run to get to the ranch along the Little Sur. The people who lived far down the coast touched civilization at King City in the Salinas Valley, another hard two-day grind east over the mountains in springless wagons.

Some of the young men found wives among the daughters on the other ranches, but there were not enough marriageable girls to go around. They tell the story of one Harlan matriarch who bragged that no schoolteacher who came down fresh from San Jose Normal College to teach in the one-room mountainside school ever got away; every one was courted and wed by Harlan sons.

Like mountain people everywhere, those of the Big Sur grew close in their isolation, proud and suspicious of strangers. They owned all the land for seventy miles along the coast, and they made sure that little of it was available to outsiders. Their isolation continued even after convicts from the state's prisons hacked and dynamited a long highway into the sides of the ocean cliffs during the two decades between World War I and the end of the Great Depression.

The land is not a hospitable one. Of the people who came seeking to make homes here, most found it difficult to come to terms with a place where winter rains could wash out roads and loose great slides to block the highway and leave a family cut off from the world; where such a simple thing as shopping for supplies meant a hundred-mile round trip to Monterey. Some were intimidated by the sheer immensity of the place and fled. The old families watched them all come and go, indifferent except when the newcomers threatened a way of life that had roots a hundred years old.

These coastal mountains offer few opportunities to earn a livelihood, although at one time or another a variety of enterprises has existed here. The hills have been mined for limestone and gold, the forests cut for timber and tanbark. There was even a coal mine in one canyon. But because of the inaccessibility of the land, it was uneconomical to ship the limestone and the coal; the demand for tanbark declined, and the veins of gold proved to be meager. One after another the operations closed down, and there was no more work. Until recently, of all those who came here, only the wealthy or those who by sheer tenacity and guts could find a way to sustain themselves stayed on.

The developers stayed away. Water was scarce, the land was not for sale, and besides, who had ever heard of the Big Sur? The tourists stayed away, too, except for a few who were in no hurry and were willing to drive the long, dangerous road from Monterey to San Luis Obispo.

Then, after World War II, the fifth and latest of the great migrations into California began—one which made the others seem insignificant —the invasion by tourists and homeseekers. Quite often the first became the second. They applied great pressure on the economy and on the available space. Opportunists jumped at the chance to turn their influx into personal bonanzas. From Oregon to Mexico, mountains were carved up for subdivisions, valleys were filled with concrete, and filling stations and supermarkets, used car lots, souvenir shops, and hamburger stands sprang up throughout California.

Even the Big Sur was affected. It changed slowly at first because it was out of the way and not readily accessible. But it was too close to the exploding population centers of the Monterey Peninsula, San Jose, the San Francisco Peninsula, and the East Bay cities to retain its isolation. What changed it more than anything else, and changed it almost overnight, was the opening of an attraction that captured the imagination of tourists from every state of the Union—San Simeon.

Just south of the point where the coast road descends from the cliffs of the Santa Lucias, a white marble palace, Graeco-Roman-Moorish in design, stands on a ridge above the long meadows. It was a monument to its builder, William Randolph Hearst. From this grandiose white edifice he ruled his far-flung newspaper empire, and here he held court like some minor oligarch.

The rooms of the palace were filled with miscellaneous art objects collected for him in Europe by squads of agents—Flemish tapestries, wood paneling from Bourbon chapels, paintings from Spain. The near great of a bygone era—the movie people, politicians, and journalists of the twenties and thirties—ate, played, and slept here, basking in the patronage of the lord of the manor. After he died, his heirs, to escape the massive taxes, gave San Simeon to the state, which promptly threw it open to the public.

It stood on its hill like an Italian fortress in Tuscany with a feudal town at its base—a dozen motels and restaurants and gift shops awaiting the tourists who poured in from everywhere. They followed guides about the palace and marveled at baronial splendor punctuated with ketchup bottles and paper napkins. Most thought it America's answer to the Louvre; a few thought it considerably less. They went away impressed in one way

or another and told their friends. Their friends came and their friends' friends, in never-ending waves down the coast highway from Monterey. The Sur was never quite the same again.

At the same time that it began to be overwhelmed by tourists, the Big Sur also became a mecca for a new breed of the young who had become alerted to its existence by Henry Miller, writing from his perch atop Partington Ridge. His followers came to see and took the word back to San Francisco, where it was heard in North Beach, haunt of the beatniks of the middle Fifties. They came in droves to the hills and canyons of the Big Sur to commune with like-minded souls and to join together to send out strange vibrations on the mountains. They were poets and mystics and bards, saints and frauds and thieves and scroungers of great accomplishment and careless verve. The people of the Big Sur for the most part recoiled in dismay, locked their gates, and barred their doors.

Even now, twenty years later, the road south from Carmel along the coast is thick with the migrant young, footloose and carefree, lumped under the catch-all term "hippie." They speak reverently of the environment, yet in their carelessness they have polluted its rivers and have twice burned the mountains bare.

They are of all sorts and persuasions. Some are as conservative as their fathers ever were; others are desperate dropouts from civilization, feral and dangerous. Most of them fall somewhere in between. But they all look the same—hair long and adrift in the wind, with a general air somewhat grubby and often faintly cloaked in the smoke of hashish. They are on the move and on the make for whatever they can get. Steinbeck, were he to walk this way today, would recognize Mac and Eddie and the boys from the Palace Flophouse and Grill on every hand.

In late afternoon the sun lays a blazing path
across the dark and restless sea . . .

. . . and in that long moment before it drops from sight, the whole coast is aflame with a radiant orange light.

THE
ELEMENTS

THE SEASONS

"In the deep spring when the grass was green on the fields and foothills, when the lupines and poppies made a splendid blue and gold earth, when the great trees awakened in yellow-green young leaves, then there was no more lovely place in the world. It was no beauty you could ignore by being used to it. It caught you in the throat in the morning and made a pain of pleasure in the pit of your stomach when the sun went down over it."

—THE WAYWARD BUS

There is a time, even before winter has departed, when the earth stirs itself and sends forth the first harbingers of the coming spring.

After the winter rains, trees are covered with new buds, and blue lupines appear everywhere across the valley.

Spring comes late on the higher, colder slopes; when the earth is turning dry, plants on the mountains put forth their blooms.

In summer, after the sun has scorched the land, dried grasses and skeletons of weeds stand lifeless in the heat.

When the rains stop in the spring, the hills along both sides of the Salinas Valley are ablaze with wild flowers: poppies, phacelias, myriad kinds of lupines, and all the other glories native to this place. In the shaded glens along the streams that flow out of the canyons into the Salinas, the iris and the mimulus are as lovely as any orchid growing in a tropical jungle. The grasses, lush and tall, cover the slopes with brilliant green.

This is a time of renewal for the land. Birds swarm, nesting in pine forest, meadow, and the chaparral of the mountain slopes, and the land is loud with the cries of quail scuttling through the underbrush. Small rattlesnakes come forth from whatever dark recesses they have inhabited during the frosty winter months.

On the valley floor, the branches of the apricots are ablaze with pink and white, a smoky veil against the dark hills beyond. All up and down the valley the farms are checkerboards of black plowed earth and green growing crops: lettuce, broccoli, celery, garlic, carrots, onions, sugar beets, corn, potatoes, strawberries, and all the other produce of this mammoth agri-business. It is perhaps the most fertile and productive land in the world.

The fields, laid out in geometrical ranks on the flatlands along the river, are combed, curried, and manicured beyond belief. Tons upon tons of chemicals are spread upon them, the air at times becoming almost unbearable with the smell of ammonia generated from nitrogen compounds in the fertilizer. Millions of gallons of water, pumped from the Salinas River or from wells that tap the water table beneath the surface, are poured onto the land.

As the crops reach the time of first harvest, Mexican field hands arrive from Texas, Arizona, and the Imperial Valley to swell the ranks of the local labor force; they work in the fields, stooping, hoeing, cutting, gathering, picking. Because of the always impending threat of labor troubles, the farmers desperately utilize every mechanical means possible to plant and harvest the crops. Yet there are things no machine can do, so people labor in the fields, either following the machines or gathering in the crops by hand in ways nearly as old as man himself.

The migrants follow the harvest up and down the valley, and when the work is slack, they move over into the San Joaquin or north into the orchards of the Santa Clara Valley, fast disappearing among the sprawling suburbs of San Jose. Such is the foresight of the migrants and the nature of their recompense that although some spend their gain as fast as it is earned, drinking and gambling, others work as family groups, small children augmenting the work of parents and older relatives; these groups bank their pay and drive from one crop to another in new cars.

Over all is the sound of transistor radios, hung on the belts of the people as they work down the rows; those of the elders lament with the traditional Mexican love songs of Augustin Lara from the Spanish-language station in King City, while those of their children are shrill with the sounds of the Grateful Dead and the Rolling Stones.

As the year goes on, the upper valley heats up and draws fog from the ocean into its lower parts so that Salinas may be a chilly 50° while forty miles away in King City the thermometer will stand at 90°, and in the side valleys the heat will go up past the 100° mark. In the heat and drying air, the earth dries rapidly, and pumps along the river work harder and longer to bring water to the land. At the two dams on the Nacimiento and San Antonio rivers in the Santa Lucia range, the engineers release enough water to keep the Salinas flowing to supply the fields.

By June, in the valley south of King City, on

Far to the east, on the dry cattle ranches of the Gabilans, the hills grow sere; what grass there is will be grazed off by September.

*In the Santa Lucias, where the madrone sheds its bark in early autumn,
poison oak stands guard against the careless traveler.*

*In the vineyards, early cold paints the grape leaves;
in a few weeks dawn will find the grasses on the
hillside stiff with frost.*

the Rancho San Lucas, on the old Rancho Pleyto near Mission San Antonio in the hills to the west, and along the Lonoak Road in the Gabilans, the fields of barley and oats are a rich gold, bearded heads heavy in the heat, awaiting the reaper and the hay baler. Cattle graze in the stubble of harvested fields. As forage grows scarce, ranchers send their steers to the feedlots at Fat City on the slopes east of Gonzales, for in the dry upland meadows where cattle and sheep are the only crop, there is little water.

In September, at the equinox, storm clouds pile up over the ocean and make their way in threatening ranks over the Santa Lucias. Occasionally, there may be thunder and lightning, and showers may fall briskly and briefly for a momentary break in the drought. But within a day or two the skies are empty and the sun beats down again on the hills and valleys of the Salinas.

The heat continues to grow in intensity. By October all of California west of the Sierra swelters in the hottest days of the year, days when stifling heat traps lethal smog over all the heavily inhabited parts of the state. In the mountains, fires rage out of control and smoke from burning forests darkens the skies.

In November cooling winds come from the north, and the first winter storms from the Gulf of Alaska begin to invade the Northwest and send scouting parties into northern and central California. At length the rains begin in earnest, and parched hills soak up the water and send the runoff pouring into empty creeks and the bottoms of the tributary valleys.

When the mercury plunges and frost lies upon the mountains and even creeps down toward the slopes that edge the sea, the rain turns to snow on the crests of the Sierra de Salinas and the Gabilans, and the sun rises on clear mornings in the valley.

Even while the rain is falling, the beginnings of next season's harvest are growing in the soaked ground, overwintering crops planted while the fields were dry. Seed supplies and fertilizers are readied, and when the rain slackens and the land is dry enough to accept the plow, the cycle will begin again, to follow in the path of a hundred seasons past, the farmer laboring mightily, one eye on the land, the other on the market.

THE DROUGHT

"And then the dry years would come, and sometimes there would be only seven or eight inches of rain. The land dried up and the grasses headed out miserably a few inches high and great bare scabby places appeared in the valley. The live oaks got a crusty look and the sagebrush was gray. The land cracked and the springs dried up and the cattle listlessly nibbled dry twigs. Then the farmers and the ranchers would be filled with disgust for the Salinas Valley. The cows would grow thin and sometimes starve to death. People would have to haul water in barrels to their farms just for drinking. Some families would sell out for nearly nothing and move away. And it never failed that during the dry years the people forgot about the rich years, and during the wet years they lost all memory of the dry years. It was always that way."

— EAST OF EDEN

There are years when the rains come late in December, fall fitfully until the end of January, and then fall no more. By the first of April, fire warnings are up in the hills; by the end of May, springs and small streams are dry, and the hills are brown. Then the worried ranchers begin to talk of conserving water as the threat of extended drought hangs over them.

Older men among them remember the stories their grandfathers told of the time a century ago, in 1871, when no rain fell at all during a seven-year span—when 75,000 head of cattle were reduced to 10,000 through starvation and thirst, and when many struggling farmers, backs against the wall and facing unmet mortgage payments, lost their land. That specter looms large again in a year of little rain, and when the year stretches to two, three, or four, worry about the level of water above the dams and in the water table grows audible. Men begin to talk about limiting the number of new wells drilled upon the land, though they know full well the law permits no such prohibition.

Far above the dams, the Nacimiento and San Antonio rivers shrink until they are no wider than a man's stride, and their waters grow cloudy with the algae that thrive in the shallows. Still, water is pumped prodigally from the Salinas, and the water level of the lakes begins to fall too low for complacence. The Arroyo Seco, normally a fast-flowing stream as it plunges down its gorge, slows to a trickle and is abruptly dry below the Wiley ranch. Its sparse waters end in a shrunken pool below a vineyard, where the hot, dry air is shattered by the loud, recorded sound of starlings in distress, played all day long to worry the flocking birds away from the new grapes.

Storage ponds in the hills grow dry and cracked in the sun, and herds are sold before their prime to a depressed market. Deer, their water and food supply gone, come down from the hills, thin and sick, their ribs showing like slats through dull, dry hides, their eyes feverish with thirst. As food grows scarce the population of mice and ground squirrels shrinks. Life becomes rigorous for the hunters in the hills—the red-tailed hawks, the weasels, badgers, skunks, foxes, and coyotes; they descend to the farms along the river in search of sustenance, and the toll along the highways and around the farmhouses reaches tragic proportions. The black vultures, gracefully sailing the currents of the sky, circle lower and lower in ever-growing numbers; they have their fill.

The rains will come again—they always have. Yet in a land utterly dependent upon the local rainfall, with a swelling urban population making heavy demands upon the same water that supplies the fields, the seeds of desperation are at hand. They may already have been planted.

When the summer sun heats the upper valley, cold fog advances from the ocean; by nightfall it has crept far inland between the ranges.

THE WIND

"In the afternoon Samuel and Adam rode over the land. The wind
came up as it did every afternoon, and the yellow dust ran into the sky.
*   " 'Oh, it's a good piece,' Samuel cried. 'It's a rare piece of land.'*
*   " 'Seems to me it's blowing away bit by bit,' Adam observed.*
*   " 'No, it's just moving over a little. You lose some to the*
James ranch but you get some from the Southeys.'
*   " 'Well, I don't like the wind. Makes me nervous.' "*

—East of Eden

In the Salinas Valley, the wind blows. It is not a gentle zephyr nor a summer breeze, but most often a brisk, searching, persistent wind that causes the unprepared to draw his neck down between hunched shoulder blades and seek out any lee to break its force.

The wind usually rises in the afternoon as air from the sea moves into the warmer valley. It starts out as a smart onshore breeze which caps the waves with curls of white and catches spume from the breakers and wafts it ashore in a thin veil over the artichoke fields near the river mouth. It moves on, past Castroville, picking up vagrant papers along the Southern Pacific tracks and sending them sailing over the lettuce fields surrounding Salinas until they end their journey piled against some distant roadside fence.

As the valley narrows between the two ranges on each side, the wind is funneled and its velocity increases. At Chualar it makes angry riffles on the surface of the river and sends the leaves of poplar trees along its banks dancing in frantic rhythm, their white undersides presenting a united front to the gale, like their cousins the quaking aspens. As the wind strikes the long ranks of eucalyptus trees below Soledad, planted decades ago to break its force, it bends them southward, their long, leathery leaves clattering in the turbulence. One of the salient features of the valley as far as San Lucas and beyond are the frequent trees, exposed to these winds, that have their branches arranged on the lee side of the trunk, as contorted by the force of these constant winds as the one-sided pines on the cliffs of Point Lobos.

The people who work in the fields come prepared against the wind, muffled to the eyes, for the wind can cut to the bone. Men riding the tractors resemble Bedouins of the desert.

When the plowed fields up against the flanks of the hills are dry, the wind picks up topsoil from the furrows and lifts it into the sky. The valley below Soledad is filled with dust until the hills disappear behind a thin, yellow veil and the soil on the ground drifts along the plowed rows like small dunes on the breast of some pygmy desert. The dust hangs in the air until the sun sets and the wind subsides.

During the hot months from June to October, the inversion layer that is usually present in California valleys wraps the upper slopes in furnace heat. When ranchers come down from pastures on the heights, bathed in sweat, they suddenly shiver in winds blowing on the valley floor, winds that can have a chill factor forty degrees lower than the air of the ridges above.

The main streets of the valley towns—Chualar, Gonzales, Soledad, Greenfield, King City—all are aligned with the axis of the valley; the wind rushes down these straightaways, cold and unrelenting. The forlorn drunks draw their ragged clothes closer and huddle with their wine bottles in the slight shelter of doorways along the streets.

During the winter and spring, winds will sometimes blow strong and icy from the northeast; these are flank columns of polar winds advancing east of the Sierra Nevada. Where these winds blow, the air in the valleys moves briskly and the valleys are swept clean of smog and dust. It is on such days as these that men climb the highest hills, Palo Escrito or Chews Ridge or Junipero Serra, to see as far into the distance as they can, a mighty compulsion in some men. From these heights they can see Mount Diablo and Mount Tamalpais standing high over San Francisco Bay; to the east lies Half Dome in Yosemite, and farther south, Mount Whitney on the crest of the snowy Sierra. But when the winds die down and the magnificent vistas fade, the haze and smoke creep back, dimming the eyes and, too often, the spirits of these far-gazing men.

The valley floor is at its loveliest in the spring, when hillsides are mantled in soft, luminous green. Cool breezes from the sea flow southward, bending the tall eucalyptus and causing a million orange poppies to dance in the sun. Along the roads meadowlarks sit on barbed wire, balanced against the wind, and spend their song upon the air. Mourning doves spring up from the fields with wings flashing white, leaving behind them small scythes of sound to please the ear. And the scent of lupine fills the air, carried to every corner of the valley by the wind.

THE FOG

"There was none of the sharp outline we think of as reality. The tree trunks were not black columns of wood, but soft and unsubstantial shadows. The patches of brush were formless and shifting in the queer light. . . . The wind arose as they walked, and drove the fog across the pale moon like a thin wash of gray water color. The moving fog gave shifting form to the forest, so that every tree crept stealthily along and the bushes moved soundlessly, like great dark cats. The treetops in the wind talked huskily, told fortunes and foretold deaths."

— TORTILLA FLAT

During the summer months, when the earth turns its northern face to the sun, the land grows hot; the sun rises out of the granite peaks of the Sierra Nevada and burns down upon the basin of the great Central Valley. The valley swelters, each day hotter than its predecessor. From Redding and Red Bluff at the foot of Mount Shasta to Weedpatch and Bakersfield beneath the Tehachapis five hundred miles to the south, the heat shimmers and pulses until the ground itself becomes a radiant body, blistering to the touch.

To a lesser degree the valleys of the Interior Coast range also grow hot, as all of California east of the ocean bakes and boils and fries day after searing day. Even the Salinas Valley does not escape. Where the river begins in the hills above Paso Robles, the summer days reach a hundred degrees for days on end. As far downstream as King City, the valley frequently is an oven.

As the heated air of the valley rises during the day, a layer of cool air from the ocean begins to move inland, carrying masses of fog into the valley of the Salinas and pressing it against the Aromas hills and the low ridges near San Juan Bautista that mark the northern limits of the valley. The bases of the two sentinels towering high on either

On some mornings the sun rises over a river of fog that fills the whole valley with deep billows of cold mist.

side of Salinas, Fremont Peak on the east and Mount Toro on the west, are enveloped in white mist. Long, exploratory streamers of fog begin to move slowly southward. The white tentacles become patches, and the patches become billows, moving steadily past Salinas and Spreckels and Chualar. At Gonzales, where cattle-feeding pens sprawl at the foot of the eastern range, the damp smell of the mist becomes pungent with ammonia as the fog slides over the huddled herds, past the penitentiary, and on down the valley to Soledad and the towns beyond.

At the same time another stream of fog moves up Carmel Valley, borne inland by a steady wind. It climbs the ridges of the Aguajito and Jacks Peak, curling up over Los Laureles, and down into Corral de Tierra. Slowly the fog piles higher against the western slopes of Mount Toro and Palo Escrito ridge until, bursting over the top in a graceful banner, it flows downward to join the white river moving silently up the Salinas Valley.

At times like these, all the northern reaches of Monterey County lie beneath a wet, billowing blanket. Only the highest ridges of the Aguajito, the hills above the Stuyvesant Fish ranch, and the tops of Toro and Fremont stand above the fog, like a chain of islands in some gray sea.

As dusk comes, puffs of fog begin to condense as little advance patrols ahead of the advancing main body; each side canyon begins to fill with wispy, gray-white mist. The Arroyo Seco, the bowl beneath the West Pinnacles, Pine Valley, and hundreds of clefts in each of the mountain walls on either side—all become white tributaries of the Salinas Valley.

Often, by the time the night is over, the long valley is a hundred-mile river of fog. Beneath this close-clinging layer, the only sound is the *purr* of water pumps and the *swish-swish* of high-pressure sprays dousing the onions, alfalfa, sugar beets, beans, and celery.

Sometimes, when the trough of the great Central Valley becomes an intolerable hell, its rising heated air affects the air currents as far away as the ocean. The fog moves far inland, filling all the coastal valleys, and climbs the last ramparts of the Interior Coast Range until it piles up in a shimmering mass atop the crests. Sometimes it hangs there for days, held at bay by blistering updrafts from the furnace to the east. Then only the highest points of land remain above the fog: Loma Prieta in the Santa Cruz mountains and pointed Pacheco Peak east of Hollister. The northern Santa Lucias lie cool and damp with only their tallest peaks poking up through the mist: Chews Ridge, Cone Peak, Pico Blanco, the Ventana Cones, and the twin giants, Pinyon Peak and Junipero Serra.

When this time comes, the people along the coast—in Moss Landing, Castroville, Monterey, and the Big Sur—shiver in the cool dampness and grumble about the weather. Sometimes, at the foggiest places on the Peninsula, in Pacific Grove or the Carmel Highlands, the fog will draw a curtain across the sun and remain for the better part of an entire summer. Then the idle affluent of the Peninsula seek out sunny places in upper Carmel Valley, while Monterey and Carmel are shuddering under the impact of thousands fleeing to the misty cool from the baking valleys of the Sacramento and the San Joaquin. The wealthy farmers and cattle ranchers of Modesto and Chowchilla and Tranquillity, the grape growers of Delano, and the cotton and potato farmers of Kern County send their wives and daughters to languish in summer homes along the green, manicured fairways of the country clubs in Del Monte Forest.

The fog settles in Monterey Harbor, and the wharves stretch out from the shore to disappear into a gray blankness. Small boats materialize from nowhere and drift through the gloom toward berths within the breakwater. Somewhere beneath the gray pall of fog, past the last rusty fishing boats rocking at anchor, the sea lions on the Coast Guard jetty converse in muted, coughing barks. The bell buoy at the end of the breakwater tolls with the measured rocking of the swells.

It is a subdued time in Monterey, a time for drawing inward. The old Sicilians in the Customhouse Plaza stop their endless boccie game and wander off up the hill toward the bright haven of home. Soldiers from Fort Ord disconsolately search out the light and warmth of the Poppy Restaurant or the Bus Depot Cafe. The prostitutes from San Francisco, their arrival in Monterey coinciding with military paydays, wander cold and forlorn on the damp sidewalks of lower Alvarado Street, walking an endless beat from one saloon to another. Even the steatopygic black hookers in their short, tight skirts lose their easy jocularity and grow morose and silent in the early dark.

Monterey shares with its sisters, Pacific Grove and Carmel, a notable restraint in the facades of its main street. Indeed, it lacks the sine qua non of any progressive, up-and-coming, self-respecting American municipality: a business district filled with the glittering splendor of flashing bulbs and neon tubing. So it is that when the fog flows gently over the ridge above the highest houses on the slope and down through the streets of Monterey, the town becomes quiet and subdued, soft, feminine, and lovely.

On Cannery Row the fog muffles the broken outlines of the sagging canneries and creeps through shattered windows, filling them with a soft, amorphous grayness. Underneath the buildings, where bums lie insentient among the pilings, the fog draws a damp blanket over sprawled, sodden bodies.

Then it is that the cats of Cannery Row, in uncounted hundreds, creep from their hiding places beneath the splintered timbers and rusted machinery to search with malevolent eyes for such natural enemies as dogs and small boys. Fierce and feral, they wander in packs behind the restaurants, where the fish scraps are dumped upon the beach and where they compete with circling, screaming gulls and with each other for every morsel. There are great gray cats, tiger-striped cats, scabrous tortoiseshells, lineal descendants of those sleek and well-fed pets kept by the girls at the Bear Flag and La Ida's. All night they range the Row, brawling, yowling, mating in the foggy dark.

On the slopes above Monterey and Cannery Row, in the pine woods where Danny and Jesus Maria Corcoran and the Pirate with his dogs used to live, the fog creeps among the trees and fills every hollow and cove. The long moss that beards the trees, the lichen on the fallen trunks and sagging fence posts, the wild huckleberry and salal become sodden in the mist; and every hanging leaf, heavy with water, looses a steady drip on the forest understory.

Sounds grow soft and muffled; the distant surf becomes no more than a murmur. Even the harsh bellow of the foghorn at Point Piños, penetrating to these upper slopes, becomes as soothing as the soft *whooo* of an owl. All things here take on the muted color and pace of the fog; all except man, and even he is dwarfed by the gray void that surrounds him.

Sometimes the fog banks pile up so high
they reach the mountain tops, slip among
the trees, and spill into the canyons beyond.

THE
PEOPLE

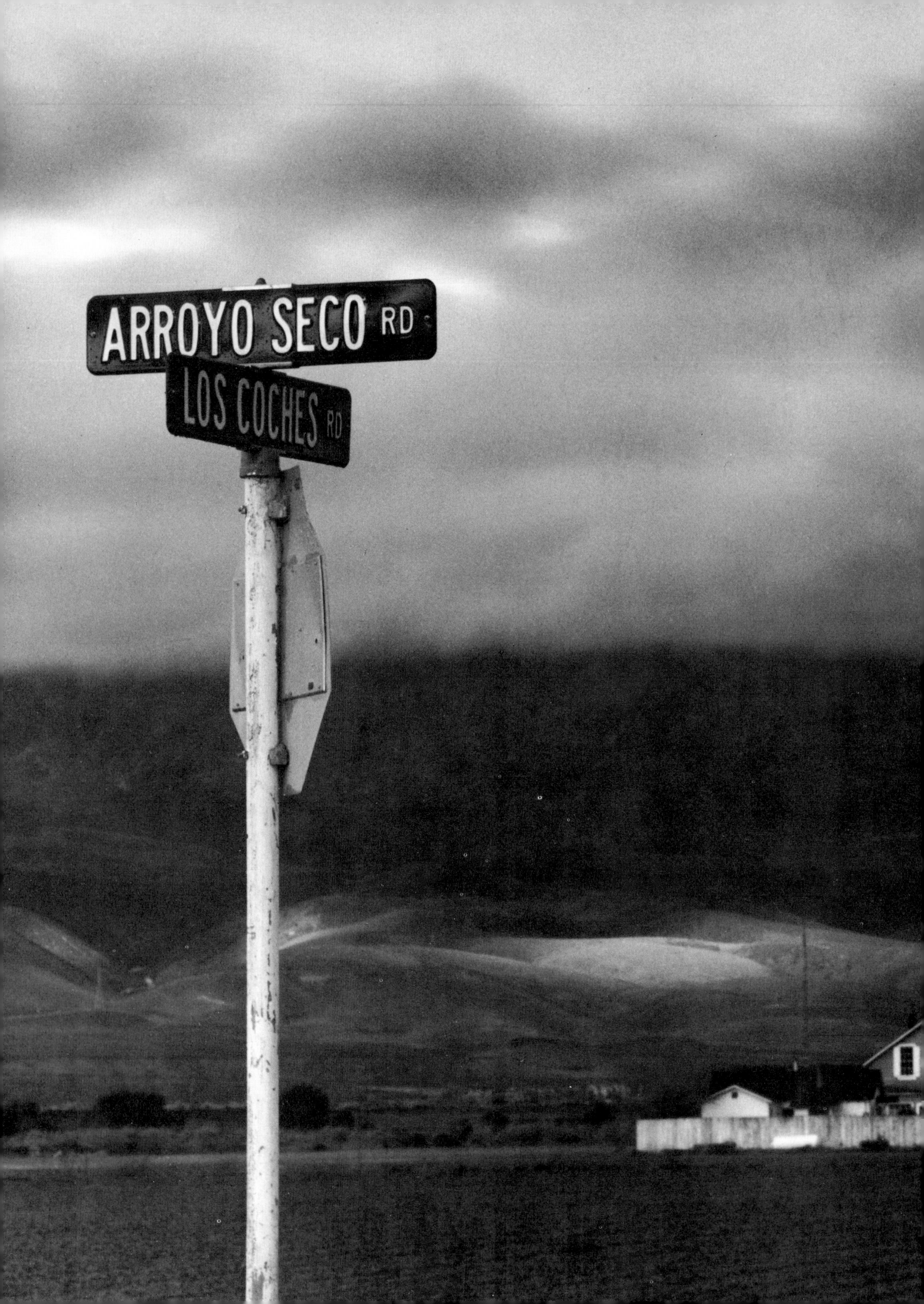
ARROYO SECO RD
LOS COCHES RD

THE SPANISH

*"When the Spaniards came they had to give everything they
saw a name. This is the first duty of any explorer—a duty and a
privilege. You must name a thing before you can note it on your
hand-drawn map. . . . The names of the places carry a charge of
the people who named them, reverent or irreverent, descriptive,
either poetic or disparaging. You can name anything San
Lorenzo, but Shirt Tail Canyon or the Lame Moor is something
quite different."*

—EAST OF EDEN

The history of these shores and valleys stretches back into respectable antiquity, as such things go in the western hemisphere. As Michelangelo lay down his brush upon completing *The Last Judgment* on the wall of the Sistine Chapel and Henry VIII was just relieving his fifth wife, Catherine Howard, of her head, Juan Cabrillo was sailing up the coast of California on the first northward journey of exploration by European seafarers; he sailed past Monterey Bay after noting La Punta de Piños, the hook at the southern tip of the bay, as a landmark on his charts. The year was 1542, only twenty-three years after Balboa had discovered the Pacific.

By 1565 Spanish galleons were sailing past regularly, bound from Manila to Acapulco, heavily laden with bullion. In 1579 Sir Francis Drake sailed along these shores in the *Golden Hind,* landed on Point Reyes, took possession in the name of England, and named the land "Nova Albion."

The first white man actually to see the bay and recognize it for what it was, was one Sebastian Cermeño, a shipwrecked explorer who was beating his way south, close to shore, in a small boat he had built from the wreckage of his galleon *San Augustin,* spent upon the rocks north of the Golden Gate. He sailed along the shore of the bay on December 10, 1595, and called it La Bahia de San Pedro.

Sebastian Vizcaíno, a merchant sea captain who had traveled the galleon trade routes, sailed his flagship *San Diego* into Monterey Bay on December 15, 1602, the second European to enter its waters and the first to step on its shores. He took possession of the land for the king of Spain.

When Vizcaíno stepped ashore on Monterey Bay, St. Augustine in Florida and Santa Fe in New Mexico were the only settlements established in what we now call the United States. The British had not yet made any permanent incursions on

*Gone are the conquerors who marched this way bearing the flag of Spain,
but the signs of their passage remain.*

the eastern seaboard. Vizcaíno proclaimed the shore of California a part of New Spain five years before the settlers stepped ashore at Jamestown and eighteen years before the weary Pilgrims reached Plymouth.

For a century and a half the Spaniards allowed Monterey to fade into the fogs of almost forgotten history. Not until they began to hear rumors of British and Russian encroachments on the shores of Alta California did they bestir themselves to look to the investiture and defense of their northern possession. They sent Gaspar de Portolá on a long journey to find and garrison the lovely bay extolled by Vizcaíno as a harbor beyond parallel, sheltered from all winds and abundantly supplied with water and game. Portolá made the long, wasting overland trek from the tip of Baja California. So extravagant had been Vizcaíno's description that Portolá did not recognize it when he found it; he went all the way to San Francisco Bay still searching for it. He returned to Mexico and came back in 1770 with settlers, soldiers, and a priestly group headed by Padre Junipero Serra. On the southern shore of Monterey Bay Portolá established a garrison, and Serra a mission.

Thus when a handful of British subjects were on the verge of setting the colonies on the Atlantic seaboard afire with revolt, Monterey was embarking on an easygoing century of Spanish and Mexican rule. Even today, the legacy of those unhurried days remains as a woof of shot gold in the rough warp of hustling Yankee commercialism.

During the course of two centuries, the men who explored, colonized, and exploited the land left their marks on it in many ways, not least in the names they affixed to landmarks, terrain features, and such. The Spanish and the Mexicans, with a touch of poetry in their souls, gave soft, charming names to the mountains and farms and rivers, names that caress the ear like gentle plashing water, names that conjure up a pleasant picture of the things of which they spoke.

At the far south of the long valley, where the ancient Camino Real passed over the last rise and weary travelers could look down on the watercourse of the Salinas, they called it the pass of the oaks, Paso Robles. The names of their saints they gave to San Lucas and San Ardo, shortened to convenience from San Bernardo. The mountain range between the valley and the sea was named after the gentle Saint Lucy; that to the east, Gabilan, for the hawks wheeling in majestic ease above its crags and peaks.

The beautiful valley lying between Mount Toro and the hills above Monterey, shaped like a great bowl nestled in the lap of the mountains, they called the corral of earth, Corral de Tierra. Steinbeck made it famous as the Pastures of Heaven, and his name comes closer to the truth.

Their ranchos they gave names both pleasing and descriptive: the ranch of the little springs, Los Ojitos; the ranch of the little gardens, Rancho Milpitas; the ranch of the marsh of the hawk, Rancho Cienega del Gavilan; the ranch at the corner of the salt marshes, Rancho Rincon de las Salinas; plain of the beautiful view, Llano Buena Vista. The list is endless, the legacy of a race that came and settled upon the land—land that was the gift of friendly governors who ignored the rights of Indians to whom it rightfully belonged. The hidalgos cherished it, enjoyed its largess with grace and sensible restraint, and lost it to a later wave of newcomers.

The early Americans and Britons and Scots who

came and elbowed the California dons aside were of a different bent. Land to them meant not a place of succor and solace but rather a negotiable commodity, a resource to be used pragmatically, to change, to alter beyond recognition if necessary to increase its value on the market. They gave their names to their surroundings, also. David Jacks, a Scottish immigrant who was the wealthiest man in this part of California during his time, was memorialized by Jacks Peak, that noble hill dividing Monterey from Carmel Valley (the Mexicans had called it the place of the little waters, Aguajito); and by Don Dahvee Park, the closest the paisanos of his day could come to Don David. This fulsome glorification was a tribute to the wealth he had amassed and ignored the fact that he was the most hated man of his time. So hated was he, in fact, that he feared to go forth among his neighbors after dark because of threats by the many whose lands he had taken—all within the law, it has been claimed, but there were those who said that the law had been twisted beyond all recognition. When the Irish demagogue and professional rabble-rouser Denis Kearney came to Monterey to agitate against the Chinese and to exploit any other cause that was presented to him, he distinguished the occasion by three words of advice he left with the citizens of the town: "Hang David Jacks."

In most cases, the old names of the ranchos were discarded and the names of the new owners came to the fore. Thus the Rancho Potrero de San Carlos, the ranch of the little pastures of Saint Charles, came in time to be known more often as the Oppenheimer Ranch; the beautiful Rancho San Jose y Sur Chiquito became the Fish Ranch, named after its present owner, Stuyvesant Fish, a descendant of that eminent early New Amsterdam patroon, Petrus Stuyvesant. In the whole expanse of Monterey County, only two ranches retain their musical Spanish names: the Marble Ranch far up Carmel Valley is still called Rancho Tularcitos, and the Salinas Valley homestead of Julius Trescony (grandson of old Alberto) is still Rancho San Lucas. Perhaps by some coincidence, both were holdings of the original Trescony.

All the other names are gone, remembered only in unread books and dusty records, forgotten by the few remaining descendants of the dons, never known to the inundating waves of latter-day immigrants. There's the sadness to it—the legacy of the Spanish and the Mexicans, those gracious ways of the first settlers, discarded, cast aside by a more determined breed as they defrauded, swindled, and married to gain possession of the land. They are all gone—the Vallejos, Soberanes, de la Guerras, Alvarados, Estradas, de la Torres, and Malarins.

Where they once owned the land as far as eye could see and beyond, the subdivisions of a harsher culture sprawl in the valley of the Salinas and on the hillsides around Monterey. Where once the lands were called Rancho Pescadero and Rancho Punta de Piños, the speculators have bulldozed the trees aside and threaded roads with names that Serra and Vizcaíno would have thought strange indeed, names such as Vista del Camino, which means "view of the road," or Via el Cammito, which means absolutely nothing at all. Or they have established new towns with such names as Del Rey Oaks, a linguistic torture.

Perhaps it may be just as well that as the beauty of the land is sacrificed for progress, the old, lovely names, no longer appropriate nor descriptive, are allowed to pass too, unknown and unlamented by the new citizens, except for a few who sometimes pause for a backward look through the curtains of the past.

HOOPTEDOODLE

" 'No,' said Mack. 'Sometimes I want a book to break loose with a bunch of hooptedoodle. The guy's writing it, give him a chance to do a little hooptedoodle. Spin up some pretty words maybe, or sing a little song with language. That's nice.' "

—Sweet Thursday

Back in the days when relations between the United States and Mexico were disturbed by the expansionist saber-rattling of President Polk, when Mexican control of Alta California was uncertain at best and Mexican bravos imbued with *aguardiente* and distaste for the *yanquis* roamed the countryside, the Americans who lived in villages up and down the California coast were not allowed to feel secure in their persons. Compounding the unrest was a continuing fear that the British would settle the problem by seizing the land—if the French did not beat them to it.

The naval forces of the various competing powers moved back and forth upon the chess-board of the Pacific, putting in at this port and that as a show of strength. Such were the alarms that flew back and forth that on the occasion when the squadron that was the Pacific Fleet was in a Mexican port, a rumor of such tenor and magnitude was spread that it reached the uneasy ear of the commander, Commodore Thomas ap Catesby Jones. The rumor had it that relations between the United States and Mexico had passed beyond the point of rupture, that hostilities had broken out along the Texas border, and that the British were preparing to pounce upon Monterey and raise the Union Jack over Alta California. This was reason enough for Jones to weigh anchor and set sail with his force immediately. He sailed into Monterey Bay on October 19, 1842, took his marines ashore, took possession of the port, and raised the American flag over the Customshouse. The alcalde and the commandante were summoned from wherever they were to be found and told that they were to administer in the name of the government in Washington and that the town was under the full protection of the might of the United States.

Commodore Jones was a gentleman officer from Virginia, steeped in the traditions and niceties of the naval service and southern courtesy; he gave strict orders as to the behavior of his men toward the people of the town. His instructions had such weight that his sailors were models of rectitude and probity. The annals of the period relate the astonishment of one shopkeeper who was asked by a marine for the loan of some sundry for one purpose or another. Fearfully, he hastened to comply. His amazement knew no bounds when later the article was returned and payment proffered for its use.

The ladies of the pueblo were treated with utmost courtesy, which must have been as much a strain upon the naval personnel as it was a relief to the locals, who had reason to mistrust all military men of whatever nationality and stripe.

Now it so happened that in Monterey were such men as Thomas Larkin, the American consul, who were privy to the thoughts and actions of official Washington. It must have been such a man who courteously led the commodore aside and informed him on the day following the seizure that the rumor he had heard in the Mexican port was false and that relations were still intact—cracked, but not shattered—between Mexico and Washington. The enormity of his mistake must have been as immediately apparent to Jones as

to his informant.

It was then that the commodore proved himself to be as adaptable and flexible in his day of trial as was Mack, the brains of the Palace Flophouse and Grill exactly a century later. Possibly the humor of the whole affair escaped Jones at the moment; at any rate, he immediately set upon a course of action as contrite as Mack's when he contemplated the horror of a welcoming party at Doc's gone wrong.

The commodore again summoned the alcalde and the commandante, delivered a persuasive apology, and with his troops drawn up in parade precision, hauled down the American flag from the Customshouse, and ran up the Mexican ensign in its place, while the drums rolled and the fleet at anchor in the bay fired a salute in honor of the occasion.

The townspeople, impressed by the demeanor and humility of the commander and the restraint of his men, turned out in holiday spirits; perhaps to celebrate the restoration of territorial integrity, but more probably because they were the type of people to whom anything was an excuse, they entertained all day and all through the next day with one *baile* after another. Larkin was bemused by the activities to the extent that he noted in a letter to a friend in the East that the officers of the fleet divided their leisure time between "hunting Deer at the edges of Town and pursuing Dears at the parties."

The festivities lasted through three tumultuous and beatific days, lasted until the final shore party staggered to the launches and was borne reluctantly to the ships lying offshore. Then Jones fired off a salvo in farewell, dipped his flag in salute, and sailed away to the cheers and tears of the townsfolk of Monterey.

Steinbeck would have loved it all.

THE MEXICANS

*"They could ride forty miles, play their guitars for a day
and night and ride forty miles home again. They staggered with
exhaustion after fifteen minutes behind a plough."*

— To a God Unknown

Tiburcio Vasquez was a man born at the wrong time. He was conceived, brought forth, and raised to young manhood at a time when his relatives and friends were being driven from their lands by Americans who were engaged in making them a dispossessed minority in their own homeland, all within the hazy limits of the law.

Had he been born a hundred years later, he would have organized a boycott, embarked upon a hunger strike, or brought a class action suit against his enemies. He would probably have generated widespread sympathy and support, and might have won his cause or at least have been elevated to the state assembly, where he would have become a member of the very Establishment he was fighting.

But in those days of "the only good Indian is a dead Indian," it was just as well said that "the only good Mexican is a dead Mexican." It was a time of the ascendancy of the Puritan ethic; the world belonged to the strong and the industrious, with the strict proviso that these inheritors of the earth must be white, Anglo-Saxon, and Protestant, the importance being in that order. Sadly, though Tiburcio Vasquez was an Aryan, there was an infusion to some degree or another of Moorish and Indian blood, and he was too dark ever to be taken for an Anglo-Saxon. And regardless of his sincerity and religious devotion, he entered the wrong door to approach his God.

He had been a daredevil and a minor hellraiser in his youth in Monterey, where he grew up in the family adobe that still stands in the shadow of Colton Hall. In his last days he told some inquiring journalists what had pushed him over the line: it was the Americans going to the Mexican bailes

*Sometimes there is a warmth, a closeness among these Mexican workers
that more prosperous men have lost.*

and fandangos, pushing the young men aside, and monopolizing the señoritas. On one such night a fight started and a local American gendarme who intervened on the side of his friends ended up dead on the floor, victim of a well-placed blade in the heart.

Tiburcio fled Monterey and hid among his people on the surrounding ranchos. He was a seven-day hero among the Mexicans, who looked on the Americans as conquerors, as indeed they were. So it was an easy step into full-fledged outlawry against the Americans.

The stories of that day were mixed. The Americans would have it that Vasquez was a bloodthirsty bastard who richly deserved the fate he finally met at the end of a rope in San Jose; the Mexicans looked upon him as a Latin Robin Hood, who tried to avoid bloodshed, was kind to his fellow Mexicans, and was, above all, their only champion against the conquest of California by the United States. That his cause was hopeless did not matter; what was important was that he provided a champion for the Mexicans when they needed one.

In those days when the protection of the law was not often extended to cover a dark-skinned *paisano,* he frequently found himself a hunted man, fair game for any quick-triggered American. Consequently, many paisanos examined their lives and their expectations, and finding the dice loaded against them, opted for banditry and rebellion.

Some of the more daring joined Vasquez in the hills where the Pinnacles stand sawtoothed along the crest of the Gabilans or in the canyons of the Panoche. Sometimes their forays carried them far north into the Mendocino country, sometimes east to Fresno and Madera, or even to the basin where the dusty village of Los Angeles lay, several days to the south. Their exploits were discussed with great heat by bankers and storekeepers and stagecoach drivers and lawmen up and down the state; but in the low adobes, where dim lamps flickered and the smell of masa and frijoles and chilis filled the air, black eyes sparkled as the tales of Tiburcio and his men were told. The Mexicans looked on Tiburcio as their own, hid him, aided him, and interposed themselves fiercely between him and his pursuers.

For the Mexicans, if we listen to a keen observer of that time, Robert Louis Stevenson, "although in the State, are out of it. They preserve a sort of international independence and keep their efforts to themselves. Only four or five years ago Vasquez, the bandit, the hunt too hot for him in other parts of California, returned to his native Monterey, and was seen publicly in her streets and saloons, fearing no man."

Vasquez had his counterparts in the lands far to the east, beyond the high mountains: Quantrill, the James boys, Cole Younger and his gang, Bill Bonney. He had no more chance of surviving than they had. Established society cannot tolerate his breed; they are hunted down and exterminated or rendered harmless by one means or another. Still, they are sometimes the only heroes available to those who feel no kinship with the society in which they are adrift.

When Vasquez was finally caught, tried, and hanged, the streets of San Jose were thick with Americans who came to see him die. And after he was cut down from the scaffold, they trooped off to the saloons to drink to the demise of Tiburcio.

But in the house of his cousin, Señora Bee, where they took his body, the wrinkled, brown, sad-eyed ones from the dusty adobes of Almaden, Guadalupe, and San Juan Bautista gathered around his body in the wooden coffin and prayed for the spirit of their vanquished champion. They comforted his weeping kin and prayed through the night and until the sun was high. At last they arose and took their leave, drawing their somber cloaks close against the stiff March winds in the valley; they left knowing that California was lost to them for good.

So all the old Mexican families faded away. The women of the landed families were courted and won by Americans, as good and cheap a way as any to gain title to their lands. The men, except for a sagacious few, gambled and drank away their lands. For the most part the Mexicans withdrew into little enclaves at the edges of the cities. They were menials. They lived, impoverished, in the barrios of Los Angeles and in shanties on farms in the San Joaquin and Salinas valleys. They were the disenfranchised, the forgotten, the invisible men.

For almost seventy-five years, the Mexicans stayed quiescent; they were resentful but resigned. During the years after World War I, Mexicans from the Southwest and from below the border began a great restless movement into the valleys of California. Because they were faceless, they drifted up and down the state, going underground in Mexican settlements to elude the border patrols and immigration inspectors. When they were caught and taken back to Mexico, they were often back across the border by night—back to where they had been caught even before their captors had made the return trip. Some ranchers say that, in the valley today, eight of every ten Mexicans over the age of twenty are wetbacks. Their children, born here, are citizens.

The Mexicans who live on the farms are moving away, displaced by machines. Most of them have become permanent residents of the valley towns, living in low-income subdivisions. They go out to work the crops when the call goes out for men. The rest of the time they draw unemployment or relief checks. When they do work, the pay is good, particularly when a complete family works —and Mexican families often muster as many as eight or ten to work. When field hands are packing lettuce or picking fruit or harvesting garlic, the roads beside the fields are lined with their new Galaxies and Furies and Pontiac Wide-Tracks. Only a few rusty jalopies are mixed with the others.

Yet, a little affluence can breed an intense yearning for more and more. As the Mexicans look around at the affluence of their time, unrest and militancy have sprung up among some of them. Heeding new heroes of the day, they loose a strident cry of "Huelga! Strike!" over the fields of the Coachella and Delano and the Salinas. The farmers, fearing labor troubles, rush to mechanization—complete mechanization. There are machines for almost every operation, and most of them do what they were designed to do. All the root crops are gathered by machine. In fields of green lima beans, task forces of combines, twenty at a time, go down the rows at a slow, steady pace, great behemoths lumbering behind the growling tractors that draw them. Some machines are imperfect and waste too much of the crop. A case in point is the clanking monster that harvests apricots. Not being able to make a competent judgment as to which fruit is ripe, which overripe, and which too green, it gathers them all into its maw. Only the ones with the first blush of ripeness can be used. The others are wasted.

But man's ingenuity is beyond belief. If the machine is imperfect, then men set out to change nature to fit the machine. At the University of California, plant breeders develop a tomato plant whose fruits all ripen simultaneously, and the problem is solved. They develop a broccoli plant whose spears all rise to the same height so the machine can gather a crop with dispatch and no waste. There is even talk of a machine, now in the process of being perfected, that will move down the rows in the lettuce fields, examine the heads by x-ray, pass over the immature and gather in the fully developed ones, pack them in boxes, and stack the boxes neatly on waiting trucks to be hauled away to the refrigerator cars of the Southern Pacific.

Still, there remains work to be done that, as yet, only human beings can do. And so whole families of Mexicans—muffled against the chill of constantly blowing winds—men in stocking caps and women in conical straw hats—are in the fields at daybreak, bending, squatting, stooping their way down the endless rows.

The tragic history of the American South seems fated to be repeated in California valleys as these brown people, volatile, unskilled, many of them unlettered, are forced off the land, their work opportunities diminished to the vanishing point. And when that time comes, these Mexican Joads and all their fellows may look again to another hero, perhaps another Tiburcio, to inflame the collective imagination and strike sparks that will set these valleys ablaze.

When there is no work in the fields, men in the camps dress in their best clothes; they stand about swapping tall tales, or if times are bad, they worry about tomorrow.

Manual labor is the only way of life for thousands of Mexicans in the fields of the Salinas Valley.

THE FARMERS

"Our ancestors, so it is implied, gathered to the invitation of a golden land and accepted the sacrament of milk and honey. This is not so. . . . This land was no gift. . . . They stole and cheated and double-crossed for it, and when they had taken a little piece, the way a fierce-hearted man ropes a wild mustang, they had then to gentle it and smooth it and make it habitable at all. Once they had a foothold, they had to defend their holdings against new waves of the restless and ferocious and hungry."

—AMERICA AND AMERICANS

The Spanish hidalgo of a century and a half ago never walked when he could jump astride his horse, rake him with his rowels, and go at a dead run from his house to his barn, or his neighbor's house, or the nearest dispensary of wine and spirits. It made no difference how far he went; to walk would have been to lose stature in the eyes of his peers, and so he rode everywhere. It was all some hidalgos ever did.

In some respects, his modern counterpart is not too different. Where the Mexican lived on his horse, resplendent with tooled Spanish saddle mounted in silver, the American goes about his rounds in a shining Ford, GMC, or Chevy pickup, sparkling with chrome and often sporting a formidable rack of rifles behind him in the cab.

Only the rationale is different. The Mexican rode because he was ill at ease on foot and because he was more than a little lazy; the American rides because he firmly believes that "time is money" and walking is a slow process, not suited to modern efficiency and time-motion equations; and because, to tell the truth, he too has grown a little lazy.

But history has proved that the American had something more going for him than the Mexican had. As the Hispano-Mexican overcame the Indian by gun and cross, the American in turn overcame the Mexican by guile, acumen, and force—and because he believed that "time is money." The Mexican had only *mañana* as a competing concept; his sense of urgency was aroused only by the sound of racing hoofbeats. It wasn't enough, and he lost out. His name is missing on the mailboxes that line the long roads stretching the length of the Salinas Valley today.

There are a few farmhouses in the valley and surrounding hills that have stood a half-century or more. They have a stability, a tenacity, a rugged permanence about them, and they seem to impart these qualities to the men who live in them.

The history of land use in this valley is as varied as the people who have lived in it. When the original half a hundred or more grants were issued by the governors of Alta California, the grantees loosed their rangy Mexican cattle on the land to forage as best they could. When the rancheros needed funds, the animals were rounded up by vaqueros and all but the breeding stock were slaughtered. The carcasses were skinned and left to rot in the sun, for the only money these ranchos earned was by selling hides, at the ridiculously low price of a dollar each, to ship captains in the hide trade. Later they paid dearly for these same hides when they came back from Boston as boots and other leather goods.

This hide trade marked the beginning of Anglo-Saxon incursion into California when Lancashireman William Hartnell, followed shortly by Scotsman Hugh McCulloch, came ashore in Monterey to act as brokers for the hides; they brought as a medium of exchange a supply of combs, buttons, shawls, and cloth for the ladies, and tobacco, guns and spirits for the men. They came prepared to buy cheap, and sell dear.

The hide trade flourished—for the merchants and the brokers. Hartnell and McCulloch, being the primary source of cash for the Spanish dons, became their confidants and close companions. They were known as "Arnel y Macala"—as close as the natives could come to these outlandish names. Hartnell further entrenched himself by courting and winning the lovely Teresa, daughter of Don Jose de la Guerra y Noriega, first citizen of Santa Barbara. Thus he was the first to enter the ranks of the landed aristocracy through the convenient door of marriage. Later his clerk David Spence did the same when he married Jose Mariano Estrada's daughter, Adelaide.

During these times before the overthrow of the Mexican government, the ranchos changed little; they continued as cattle preserves with inferior herds roaming from one unfenced range to another, the brands being the only means of telling a San Lorenzo yearling from a San Bernardo or Tularcitos one.

When statehood came, the Americans got away with the most blatant example of expropriation that the continent had seen since Cortez stole Mexico from Montezuma and the Aztecs. Under the Treaty of Guadalupe Hidalgo, which brought California into the Union, the American government specifically promised that private property rights were to be safeguarded. Congress passed a law shortly after—perhaps because of misinformation, perhaps because of private urging—setting up a land commission to review all claims based on Spanish and Mexican grants.

The Mexicans were required to appear before the commission to present evidence of the validity of their claims. But therein lay the difficulty. The Mexican did business on the basis of a handshake and a promise, a more valid contract to him than a document issued by the governor—a piece of paper which had been mislaid as often as not. So it

The farmers of the Salinas Valley are astute business men; they know their job, and they know every inch of their land. They have made their valley perhaps the most productive land on earth.

was that these pleaders appeared before the commission as no more than that: pleaders. They had only their word against that of the Americans who were claiming the same land. More often than not the Americans, being wiser in such matters, pulled certain strings and crossed certain palms so that their claims were upheld. The former owners were reduced to the status of tenants or laborers, or were chased off as trespassers.

The Americans, once in firm control of the land, wasted no time on fandangos and fiestas or cattle hides staked out in the sun to dry. The land was there to be used, to produce, to make its owner rich, and for no other reason. (They, in common with settlers and pioneers everywhere, had no particular feeling for the land. This is something left for the second or third generation after land fever has subsided.) So every tillable acre in the lower valley was put to the plow and planted in wheat, barley, oats, or any other crop that promised a quick return on investment. Cattle were relegated to the upland slopes and to areas too dry to farm. Even the lack of water was overcome when irrigation ditches brought the Salinas to the fields.

The real boom started when Claus Spreckels built a sugar refinery near Salinas, having first made sure to bind a number of local farmers to an agreement to plant sugar beets and to sell the crop to him—enough farmers to plant 25,000 acres of sugar beets annually. For the farmers, here was a cash crop beyond compare—no speculation, no unsold surplus; the refinery bought the entire agreed-upon crop each year.

By the turn of the century, cattle and sheep had been relegated to a lesser place in the economy of the valley. All the flat bottomlands from King City to the sea were planted in row crops—beans, corn, tomatoes, celery for all the tables of California. The railroad had long since come to the valley,

and crops could be shipped quickly to expanding markets up and down the coast.

From these beginnings, farmers pursued a speculative course (except for sugar beets), for they dealt in crops destined for a distant market rather than for their own or local use. The methods they used to determine what they would plant were as diverse as the men themselves: some relied on their own intuition, some consulted expert advice, some called on whatever Power they thought to be in charge of their particular destinies. In the end it was all the same. If a man planted garlic and no one else did, his rewards were immediate and immense. If, on the other hand, all the others thought to plant the same commodity, all went down together, drowning in a glutted market.

Fortunately, hunches or advice or divine guidance varied enough that some middle ground was usually reached, and the crops were harvested and sold for a profit. All the same, failures were frequent enough in this sort of gambling that many small operators found themselves flat broke, and their lands passed under the sheriff's hammer to the big land buyers.

In time practically all the marginal farmers were eliminated, and their lands became part of larger and more successful farms. Yet the richness of the land was so great that it was a constant lure for newcomers to buy pieces from these large landholders, putting down all the cash they had and signing heavy mortgages for the balance. It was a hazardous life with the small farmer ground between the uncertainties of the market and the certainty of a due date on the mortgage.

Eventually some astute dreamer with an eye to the big chance thought of filling a railroad car with perishables and ice, and shipping them across the whole of America to the eastern market. On that day agriculture in the Salinas Valley went beyond the concept of producing for a regional

In the fading eyes of old men on the land are reflected the pleasures
and the vicissitudes of a life spent close to the soil.

market, and the foundations of today's mammoth agri-business were laid.

Huge profits were the reward for the grower who could put his crop in New York and Chicago and Boston at the peak of the market. As soon as a crop was ready for harvest, it was gathered, packed in ice, and shipped in the yellow cars of the Pacific Fruit Express to the East. And after a field was harvested, not one day could the land lie fallow. It was immediately put to the plow, and the seed was sown for the next crop. Sometimes as many as three crops a year could be coaxed from the same piece of land. The whole operation had the efficiency of a factory assembly line, and indeed the term "factory farm" came to be applied.

There was only one hitch in this smooth flow from plow to market. The crops had to be thinned, weeded, and gathered by hand. This required an abundant supply of unskilled labor—"stoop labor," it was called. It was performed mostly by Mexicans or Filipinos or poor whites who followed the harvests. Until Wall Street took its resounding plunge in 1929 and carried the whole country down with it, the valley had prospered well enough by these methods.

The crash brought havoc across the land without respect for class or financial standing. The poor were affected least; bad times merely meant a smaller slice of little enough to begin with. But the middle class was affected to an enormous degree, and the farmers of the Salinas Valley were firmly entrenched in the middle and upper brackets of the middle class.

As often happens when men feel a threat to their way of life, the worst in some of the farmers came out. It may be that they were forced to it by economic straits; it may even be that some of them took perverse pleasure in what they did. Whatever their motivation, in order to reduce costs, the agri-industrialists once again employed a tactic that had become traditional with them— seeking a cheaper source of labor so as to play one hungry man against another and force the wages for a day's work as low as possible. They looked once more beyond the borders of California and discovered a ready-made supply of such labor.

While the depression was deepening and the desperation of a large proportion of the citizenry increasing, there was another kind of upheaval half a continent away on the shortgrass plains. Fifteen years before, at the time of World War I, great tracts of land that had never seen the plow had been planted in wheat, and the land had never been returned to its original state. Then came a time when the winds blew with unending fury out of the west. These persistent winds lifted the soil from the dry, plowed fields and filled the air with dirt and dust for days. The fields were stripped down to the subsoil. Gray drifts piled against fence rows like snow after a winter storm. The choking dust forced itself around every door and window, and between the boards of houses. A thin layer of grit lay like a blanket upon everything the eye encompassed.

Crops were put in the ground and as promptly blew away. The people of the land hung on grimly; at first banks advanced loans, until all hope of recovery was lost. The law was busy with seizures and forfeitures. Men without a dime between themselves and the future watched their children slowly starving. Desperate, they were ready for anything that would offer even the glimmer of a chance for something better.

The story goes that agents of the California farmers went among these men dulled by hunger and hopelessness and told the story of a land of plenty in the West, where work in the fields was plentiful and food grew in riotous abundance. In this there was truth, yet the immediate results were tragic.

For thousands of Joads—mothers and fathers, sons and daughters, uncles, cousins, and brothers—piled their tattered belongings high on creaking flatbed trucks and began the hard trek from the dust-blown fields to the Promised Land. These dispossessed farmers and sharecroppers were not the only ones to join the parade. Thousands of ruined small businessmen, their stores long since boarded up, went with them.

Month after month the flood of migrants poured into California. There had been nothing like it since the days of '49 when goldseekers had stampeded into the state. They poured across the Colorado at Needles and crawled across the Mojave into Los Angeles and the orange groves. Some turned north across the Tehachapis and went into the great valleys of the San Joaquin and the Sacramento. They crossed the intervening ranges into the Salinas and Santa Clara and Sonoma valleys. Every corner of the state felt their disturbing presence.

After the first few hundred came, the farmers were beset by fear, for they remembered how their own fathers had come into possession of the land; they feared desperate, land-hungry men who might do to them what their fathers and grandfathers had done to the Mexicans who first owned these acres. Having no intention of allowing any historical repetition, the farmers met the migrants with anger, hate, intimidation, and force.

The desperate ones from Texas and Oklahoma, from Arkansas and Colorado and Kansas—all lumped together as "Okies"—were pushed and shoved and harried from one place to another, their Hoovervilles under siege, their sons beaten and jailed, to prevent any remote chance that any of them might gain squatter's rights through occupation of the land.

But they held on, and by the end of the decade, most of them had put down roots of a sort. Whole new towns grew up peopled by the migrants—Alisal and Seaside and Pajaro and Freedom—towns where even today the predominant manner of speaking is the flat, nasal drawl of Oklahoma and West Texas.

Their young men became valuable on the farms because they had a natural tinkering ability, probably the heritage of forty years of coaxing a few more miles from wheezing Model T Fords. With pliers, screwdriver, crowbar, hammer, and an unlimited supply of baling wire, they could make any machine work. They found jobs as truck drivers and tractor operators.

Some of the migrants made enough of a stake to go back to the Midwest and buy land there, completing a circle started in the worst of times and ending in the best. Others bought land in the Salinas and other valleys as it became available. They were shrewd, industrious, and conservative with their money. They prospered as the valley prospered. In time they became indistinguishable from all the other farmers except for a certain way of talking which set them apart.

They, along with Japanese returning from the beachheads of Italy and the concentration camps of America, joined the native Californians when the war ended, and they nursed, cajoled, and pampered the Salinas Valley into becoming a great green cornucopia. It has rewarded them well, all of them: the Anglo-Saxons, the Swiss-Italians, the Japanese, the Danes, the Basques.

Thus it has been that over the years the valley has been the province of many men, from those Indians at one extreme who literally looked upon themselves as children of the earth and treated the land with great fear and respect, to the men at the other extreme who looked upon it as a chattel, worthless unless producing wealth of some measurable kind. Yet, beyond a doubt the sons of some of these men have feelings different from those of their forefathers. As sometimes happens when the land fever abates, men see more clearly the land about them, and a sense of the totality of things becomes a part of their being. Talk to some of them, and you will find among them those who oppose the extermination of the mountain lion, feeling that the occasional sheep or calf they might lose is expendable to keep this magnificent predator alive. Talk to the men whose eyes light up as they look upon their land and tell you about the sweetness of its soil and its water, and about the animals and birds that live in the brush, undisturbed and unmolested.

Consider the old gentleman rancher whose house, more than a century old, an oasis in a dry canyon, is surrounded by hundreds of saltbushes he has planted solely to provide a cover for the quail he loves. When he throws out grain upon the ground in the waning afternoon, his friends flock in by the literal thousands until his yard becomes a moving, beating, pulsating carpet of feathers and plumes.

Listen to another, a man who was born and has lived all his life on a ranch here, as did his father and his father's father. He said quietly one day as he watched a magnificent buck cross the shoulder of a hill in the late afternoon light, "We don't much like to hunt them. They have as much right here as any of us; the land was theirs before men first came. My father taught me the land isn't really ours anyway. What we pay for it is just the cost for the privilege of taking care of the land while we live here."

If such sentiments and thoughts were to be generally held, unlikely as that possibility may be, who knows what might happen? The long valley might become again what it was in the beginning: a place where man is a privileged guest, where the land will nourish and cherish him as he nourishes and cherishes the land.

There are machines to harvest many crops, but some must still be gathered in ways as old as man himself.

*When the fruit ripens, women come out
from the towns to work beside their men.*

Stoop labor is left to the Mexicans; the Filipinos who used to do it are gone, and the whites won't bend that much.

Great, lumbering machines move through the fields at harvest time—cutting, picking, digging, thrashing—and work for the unskilled grows scarcer each year.

Cattle is the cash crop of the ranches
in the hills, where it takes many acres
to support a single animal.

Some ranches have been in existence for more than a century—relics of an earlier time and a source of pride today.

Some old barns and outbuildings are
falling into ruin, the families gone, their
farms made part of larger farms.

*There are still cowboys on the
ranches, horsemen quick with a rope
and handy with a branding iron.*

THE CHINESE

*"But in the dawn, during that time when the street light has
been turned off and the daylight has not come, the old Chinaman
crept out from among the piles, crossed the beach and the street.
His wicker basket was heavy and wet and dripping now. His loose
sole flap-flapped on the street. He went up the hill to the second
street, went through a gate in a high board fence and was not seen
again until evening. People, sleeping, heard his flapping shoe
go by and they awakened for a moment. It had been happening for
years but no one ever got used to him. Some people thought he
was God and very old people thought he was Death, and children
thought he was a very funny old Chinaman, as children always
think anything old and strange is funny. But the children did not
taunt him or shout at him as they should for he carried a little
cloud of fear about with him."*

— CANNERY ROW

Where once were whole companies of Chinese, now there is only Pon Chung.

The first to cast their nets gainfully upon the waters of Monterey Bay were a company of Chinese, probably a remnant of the vast number brought from China to hammer and claw a road-bed for the Central Pacific through the granite spine of the Sierra Nevada. Cast adrift by their white overlords when the last, golden spike was driven, most of them made their way to San Francisco to join the tongs on Dupont Gai. The ones who came to Monterey were no doubt fishermen by tradition and training, descendants of a hundred generations who had fished the continental shelf along the southern coast of China.

They built fishing junks and sampans, copies of those plying the rivers and coasts of their home-land, and these became a common sight in Monterey Bay. Each had eyes painted at the bow (else how could they see where to go?). The Chinese were adept at their craft; their fish traps, carefully set and tended, took a heavy yield from the sea.

Their market was not in Monterey but in the shops of Chinatown in San Francisco and even in China itself. A portion of their daily catch went north to the city, a few fish were hawked on the streets of Monterey, and the rest were spread in great drying racks around their village where the canneries now stand. The dried fish were packed in bags, and at regular intervals great Chinese junks with ribbed sails would arrive from across the Pacific and take on tons of dried squid for transport to China.

The drying racks were a source of friction between the Chinese and the burghers of Monterey. Drying fish rotted; the stink became an abomination, and the innate prejudice of the Californians against Orientals rose to a high pitch because of it. Newspapers railed against them; gangs of bullyboys cornered them and cut off

their queues. Still they persisted, their harvest from the sea growing ever more plentiful. They discovered abalone lurking on the offshore rocks and developed a method for retrieving them. The flesh they boiled long and persistently to make a soup; the shells they shipped to an eager market where they were polished and sold to sit gleaming in nacreous splendor on midwestern mantels.

The Chinese took their staple crop, squid, at night, as did the Italians later when they fished for sardines. Their boats formed a procession in the early evening as they put out to sea, each with a fire of pitch logs burning briskly in a rack at the side of the boat. Thus the fish were attracted and could be seen. The glow on the waters must have been a major tourist attraction of that day.

They cast their nets into the sea and hauled in fish by the ton: salmon, cod, sea bass, perch, flounder, sardine, octopus, anchovy, ray, and shark. The practical Chinese found a use for all; those that could not be sold for food were dried, bagged, and sold for fertilizer.

Their nets set in the bay, the boats lingered near. When by the light of their fires or the phospho-rescence of the fish they could see the schools hesitating, fearful of the nets, the fishermen would yell, and scream dreadful imprecations, and drum with sticks upon the sides of their boats. The fish, not being prepared for such shock treatment, surged into the nets to be hauled in and dumped upon the decks. When holds were full, the sam-pans made their way back to Monterey, their catch to be gutted and cleaned or spread upon the controversial drying racks.

Chinatown in Monterey was San Francisco's Chinatown in microcosm; the population was made up of companies, or tongs—the Sun Sing Company, the Man Lee Company, the Yet Lee, the Man Sing. Work was organized so that every able-bodied man, woman, and child toiled in the communal effort. Chinese fish merchants trod the streets of Monterey with baskets suspended from each end of a pole balanced delicately on their shoulders; women and children spread the trash fish to dry.

Their village also had other establishments, foreign to Monterey and Pacific Grove, those disapproving towns on either side. There were opium dens, places where dreams and surcease were for sale in open-fronted shacks, where bodies lay insensate with *yen shi* pipes dropped from slackened hands. There was a joss house where incense burned, and food and drink could be offered the hungry god who lived on the premises; where, after appropriate ceremony, prayers could be answered to guide the petitioner to the correct spot to cast his net, or the correct manner to discipline an unruly wife. His answer lay in how the joss sticks fell when tossed and how they were interpreted by the resident priest—as reliable a method as consulting the stars, peering at leaves in a teacup, or seeking the advice of a stockbroker.

The Chinese of that time were as greedily efficient as the Italians who came later; both used their skills to thoroughly deplete their fishing grounds. The Chinese, in a rapacious rush to glean the harvest of the sea in its entirety, used nets with a mesh as fine as window screens. Toward the end of their dominance of the fishing industry, they were taking fingerlings no longer than the width of a man's hand. The larger fish had long since been converted into fertilizer.

In time the Chinese disappeared from Monterey, and their village with them. Where it once was, the lonely, abandoned canneries stand, now in their turn awaiting obliteration.

"And the cool bay wind blew in through the broken windows. It was then that someone lighted the twenty-five-foot string of firecrackers."

— CANNERY ROW

Along the streets of Carmel any evening at dusk, when the light fades into twilight through the pine trees and street lights glow faintly through thickening fog, comes a gentle shuffle of footsteps along the wet pavements. Presently out of the gloom will appear the slight form and benign face of one of the last links with Carmel's historic past, Pon Chung, he of the illustrious moustache and twinkling black eyes. Or you may see him in the early morning under the Presidio hill in Monterey, where Lighthouse Avenue makes its curving way around the shoulder of the bluff just before Cannery Row splits off toward the sea. He lives here in Monterey within a stone's throw of the place where Chinese fishermen of a century ago built their village on the shore, but his heart lives in Carmel, lives on as in those days when he was a crony of Harry Leon Wilson, Lincoln Steffens, and the rest of the bohemian company that once frequented Carmel.

Pon's peregrinations brought him to Carmel from his native Canton well over half a century ago. He adopted it as his own and was, in turn, immediately adopted by its citizens, who recognized him as a kindred spirit, Carmel in those days being a haunt of offhand intellectuals and eccentric souls, rather than a congeries of boutique keepers.

They tell some lovely stories about Pon Chung. Some may even be a little true—who can tell?— for Pon, when questioned, only shrugs and smiles.

They tell how he came to be a full-fledged member of the volunteer fire department. One bright morning, so it is said, the house of Pon Wi, Pon Chung's illustrious father, caught fire. In his native China on such an occasion the householder would run posthaste to the nearest firehouse and employ the firemen to fight the blaze, the payment to be in proportion to the efficiency with which the fire was extinguished. In this instance the fire department was summoned to Pon Wi's house and proved to be most efficient. But when Pon Wi reached into his capacious sleeve to discharge his indebtedness, he was astonished to learn that in America this noble act is a courtesy of the city. In a magnificent burst of gratitude, Pon Wi is said to have presented his son to the fire department.

Another tale has it that when the fire department, volunteers to the man, arrived at the scene of a fire, Pon Chung had often preceded them and had the fire well on the way toward being in hand. The obvious solution was to fit him out with a uniform and pin a fireman's badge on his chest. This was duly accomplished with fitting ceremonies and speeches, and until the day of his honorable retirement, he rode to the fires in style, ringing the bell of the fire truck, moustaches streaming in the wind—a veritable Chinese firecracker.

A third account, which tells of Pon's devotion to duty as a fireman, comes from an old and venerated citizen of the community, whose veracity is assumed to be beyond reproach. It appears that a frantic lady called to report a blaze in her home. In due course, the entire fire department arrived in a cacophony of bells and sirens and barking dogs and small boys. The half-dozen firemen quickly disposed of two blazing towels that had caught fire from a gas range in the kitchen. After cleaning up the mess, the firemen had returned to their truck to depart when it was noticed that Pon Chung was missing. After a quick search of the premises, the awestruck searching party glanced upward to find Pon, axe in hand, neatly and efficiently chopping a man-sized hole through the shake roof.

A legend of that time holds that a greatly admired young woman of the community, one Ruth McElroy, was having a birthday and there was to be a great party to mark the occasion. Pon Chung was assisting one of his countrymen in preparation of the food. The two decided that they, too, should make some contribution to the festive day. One of them would make a cake, and the other would assume the privilege of decorating it. So Pon Chung borrowed the cone-shaped decorator from a bakery, then hurried back to his kitchen and squeezed out the appropriate pink words on the top of the cake. A beaming Pon, flanked by his friend, triumphantly bore the resplendent offering into the dining room and set it forth before the delighted guests. The words spelled out in frosting on the top: "Miss Ruth's Bath Day."

As to his personal life, Pon was reluctant to speak. Any reference to it would result in the vague uncertainty peculiar to his race when confronted with brusque Occidental inquisitiveness. It was thought that he had sons in Canton and that his wife was dead. Therefore, it was a source of great surprise when he announced one day that he wanted to arrange the passage of his family to this country from Hong Kong, whence they had made their way from unfriendly territory. To expedite the matter, records were examined to establish his citizenship, and he was found to be an alien, a fact highly embarrassing to the election board where he had been casting his vote regularly for years.

The entire community was aroused. The *Monterey Peninsula Herald* ran editorials. Petitions were circulated. The way was cleared to set the machinery of the law in motion to bestow the mantle of citizenship upon him. At length it was done, and his family was summoned from Hong Kong. A delegation of his fellow citizens went with him to meet the plane at the Monterey airport on the appointed day, and Pon's wife descended, followed by a single son whom Pon had never seen, having made the arrangements some forty years before during a short visit to his homeland.

Today, Pon janitors and he gardens. In the old days he would spend his evenings in some smoky place with his cronies, deep in a game of pinochle. He once won a whiskey decanter as a prize, playing that most unoriental of games—bridge. But most of the time when he is not working, he strolls unhurriedly about the streets of Monterey and Carmel, poking curiously into nooks and crannies, pausing now and then to pass the time of day with some old friend, punctuating his remarks with gestures of his old black pipe (filled with tobacco that has been aged and aged, then soaked in oil for a palate not conceived in the western world).

His mere presence in this time and place marks one of the last lingering ties with the days before onrushing mercantilism became the dominant way of life. This small, gentle man will take his place in history with those others who have sojourned here and have left their mark behind—George Sterling and Jack London, Mary Austin and Doc Ricketts, and the boys of the Palace Flophouse.

As the boats make for the fishing grounds off Big Sur, their wakes form blue ridges in the water to match the distant ridges of the land.

THE FISHERMEN

*"We went to the pier and looked at boats, watched them tied to
their buoys behind the breakwater—the dirty boats and the clean
painted boats, each one stamped with the personality of its
owner. . . . If the stays were rusting and the deck unwashed, paint
scraped off and lines piled carelessly, there was no need to see the
master; we knew him. And if the lines were coiled and the cables
greased and the little luxury of deer horns nailed to the crow's nest,
there was no need to see that owner either. There were deer horns on
many of the crow's nests, and when we asked why, we were told
that they brought good luck. Out of some ancient time, they
brought good luck to these people, most of them out of Sicily. . . .
If you ask, 'Where does the idea come from?' the owner will say,
'It brings good luck, we always put them on.' And a thousand
years ago the horns were on the masts and brought good luck,
and probably when the ships of Carthage and Tyre put into the
harbors of Sicily, the horns were on the mastheads and brought
good luck and no one knew why."*

— THE LOG FROM THE SEA OF CORTEZ

The sea is the only way of life these tough Sicilians know.

Late in the nineteenth century a migration of Sicilian and Neapolitan fishermen came, drawn by the plentitude of sea life in Monterey Bay. Some came from the Italian colonies at Pittsburg on the Sacramento, some from San Francisco, others from Europe, from Sorrento and Isola de Femine, summoned by sons, brothers, and cousins in California.

The fishermen soon discovered in the bay a larger cash crop than the bass, cod, and halibut brought in by the small launches and sailing boats for the fish markets ashore, much larger, even, than the salmon brought in for the lone cannery on the beach. Sardines, schools of them by the uncounted and uncountable millions, filled the bay and the nearby coastal waters. One of the fishermen, one Ferrante, more farsighted than his neighbors, thought to bring this bonanza in for export. Remembering the lampara nets used in his native Italy, he tried them on the sardines. Overnight he revolutionized the industry. Purse seiners like those in the Tyrrhenian Sea between Sicily and Sardinia, big enough to hold the huge catches, filled the harbor at Monterey.

As the number of men and boats increased, the quiet harbor exploded into ordered turmoil, and the town became geared to the pulse and needs of the fishing fleet. When the moon waxed full, the fleet rested, its nets stretched on the streets of the town to dry while the older men repaired the rips and tears. Masses were said for the repose of those lost at sea. Young girls were pursued, marriages performed, and families established. When the moon waned, skiffs and dories sculled back and forth between the seiners. Supplies were loaded and nets arranged on whaleback decks ready for use as the crews prepared the boats for the crucial dark of the moon, the only time when successful pursuit of the sardine was possible.

Came the time, and the purse seiners slipped out of the harbor at sunset, each with a lookout atop the mast. As the boats cruised the bay in circles, the crews sat below, eating, drinking, sleeping. Some time during the night, or maybe twice or three times if they were lucky, a frantic hail came from the lookout, who had spotted the glittering phosphorescence of a school of sardines in the blackness of the night. Then two of the crew dropped into the skiff astern with one end of the long net. They bobbed there alone, a lantern in the bow casting a dim glow in the blackness, while the seiner drew away, the crew playing out the nets, to make a long circle around the school, easily visible in the dark. At last they closed in on the skiff, and the net was gathered together and drawn tight like a purse, growing ever smaller. The fish, trapped in the net by the hundreds of thousands, were forced into a small, compact mass. The winches lifted the sagging net clear of the water and dropped its silvery load into the waiting hold.

With the dawn, the seiners rolled heavily home, low in the water, with sometimes a hundred tons of fish aboard each boat after an exceptional night.

Crews exult in being first to port, first to unload their catch on the wharf, while unluckier boats are left far behind, still hauling in their nets.

CANNERY ROW

*"The canneries themselves fought the war by getting the limit
taken off fish and catching them all. It was done for patriotic reasons,
but that didn't bring the fish back. As with the oysters in Alice,
'They'd eaten every one.' It was the same noble impulse that
stripped the forests of the West and right now is pumping water
out of California's earth faster than it can rain back in. When the
desert comes, people will be sad; just as Cannery Row was sad
when all the pilchards were caught and canned and eaten. The
pearl-gray canneries of corrugated iron were silent and a pacing
watchman was their only life. The street that once roared with
trucks was quiet and empty."*

— SWEET THURSDAY

To process this beneficence from the sea, Cannery Row came into being, a mile-long line of wooden factories, all anchored solidly to the street at their fronts while the rest of them sat on great wood and steel pilings above the surf. During heavy seas the buildings shuddered and creaked under the assault of the waves like wooden ships caught in a storm.

On days when boats brought fish to the canneries, their penetrating smell settled over the whole area, wafting up and down the Row as the excess catch was reduced to fish oil, meal, and fertilizer in the reduction plants. When the breeze was right, which was almost always, the stink drifted slowly toward Monterey; it curled around the point below the Presidio and on past the Coast Guard station, sending delicate tendrils of piquant scent up the full length of Alvarado Street and leaving a trail of wrinkled, upturned noses. On rare occasions the subtle aroma of overripe sardine would find its way over the hill and through the pines to the aristocratic nostrils of Carmel.

From up and down the coast and from the valleys beyond the mountains, the people came to work in the canneries. The Portuguese came, the Italians, the Japanese and Chinese and Mexicans, and they invested the street with a polyglottal clamor. The Row embraced them all.

The people who worked in the canneries separated themselves into their own subcommunities

*High above the beach, the abandoned canneries stand quiet,
deserted, and forlorn—the only visible legacy of an era
that vanished with the sardine.*

in an area west of the Presidio that came to be known as New Monterey. They lived in small enclaves on the long hillside that starts at the Southern Pacific tracks beside the canneries and rises steeply to the distant pine forest on the upper slopes of the ridge. The paisanos, that happy amalgam of Mexican, Indian, Spanish, and Anglo-Saxon blood, sons and grandsons of the first settlers, lived on the other side of the Presidio, on the hillsides above Monterey. All of them lived within the sound of the cannery whistles.

During the time of the year when sardines were plentiful, the fleet would sail into Monterey in the foggy dawn. The boats that had not been fortunate were silent and their crews morose as they sailed past the canneries and on to anchor in the harbor. The other boats, with tons of fish aboard, approached the canneries with boasting whistles. The various canneries replied, raising their voices in a hoarse chorus of welcome. Each whistle was pitched differently from all the others so that when the sounds went forth toward Pacific Grove or east around the shoulder of the hill toward Monterey or straight up the slope to New Monterey, the listening people knew immediately which canneries were receiving fish from the boats nuzzling at the hoppers in the sea behind them.

The whistles marked the limits of time for the people more than the rising or setting of the sun; the whole rhythm of the community was attuned to their sound. When they bellowed, the people dropped what they were doing and came quickly down the hill, homing on the sound. They started singly, joining others on the paths through the trees and between the houses, each group flowing into larger platoons of rubber-coated, rubber-booted men and women who poured across Lighthouse Avenue, down through vacant lots, and around the shacks along the railroad tracks. They trooped noisily past the quiet, shuttered bulk of Flora Wood's sporting house and its sister establishment down the street, La Ida's, and across Ocean View Avenue into the warm, steaming, odorous caverns of the canneries, where fish unloaded from the seiners already filled the holding vats to overflowing.

When the women were gathered and poised over the long cutting tables, the buildings shuddered and machinery began to turn long steel belts that brought the fish pouring forth in a cascade. The women bent to the endless task; fish were beheaded, trimmed, drawn, and quartered. The silver stream came on relentlessly; there was no time to draw back, to look away, lest the inundation by the torrent be irreversible. As soon as a fish was cleaned, it was stuffed neatly with its brothers into an open can that, full to overflowing, was placed upon the moving belt. It was carried away, filled with tomato sauce or olive oil, cooked in ovens, and then sealed tight by a clattering, whirling machine served by a crew of men with an endless supply of lids.

Steam rose from leaking pipes and ovens, as if fog from the gray ocean had crept inside to insinuate itself into every corner. A pervading clatter came from metal chutes where never-ending columns of cans rolled down from an inexhaustible source in some unseen loft.

Hour after hour the fish came down, knives flicked at fish, cans clattered, steam hissed and eddied over everything, until someone of authority blew a whistle to bring about a frenzied pause: stretching, smoking, chewing, gossiping. Then another whistle began the Chaplinesque dance all over again, until at last the holding tanks were emptied and the last fish moved down the table to be neatly cut up, stuffed in its can, and started on its way to an unknown table.

Up and down the Row, as this time came at each cannery, its whistle blew once more and the people moved past the time clocks into the streets and began their slow exodus up the hill. Back inside, the maintenance crew washed down the tables and floors, flushing unusable residue out through hatchways that opened upon the sea. The waiting gulls, scavengers of the shoreline, came plunging and screaming toward the scraps as they fell to the water below. The canneries slowly grew quiet, waiting until once again the whistles from a triumphant fleet set the whole town in motion.

The seasons came and went, sardines by the billion were served up by the sea, disappeared into the canneries, and then departed, wrapped in tin and neatly stacked, case on case, in truck and boxcar. Until, in time, the boats came silently back into the harbor more often empty than full. The crews blamed their luck on everything except the obvious: there were no more sardines.

Eventually the purse seiners moved south to Port Hueneme, San Pedro, San Diego, and some went on halfway around the world to fishing grounds off West Africa. They never returned; there was no reason to. The sardines were gone, disappeared as completely as if they had never existed in the bay.

The canneries on the Row fell silent and empty, all save one, which still sporadically canned mackerel, anchovies, and squid. The rest stood there quiet, deserted, forlorn, the wind whistling through their empty windows. Finally, the last cannery closed its door and an era came to an end.

In the decade and a half since the sardines disappeared and the whistles fell silent, the people of the hillside above the Row have turned to other things. Some work for the army at Fort Ord; some fish for the tourist dollar as relentlessly as they used to pursue the sardine. Some have even fashioned a career built on the firm, secure foundation of a regular welfare check. The poorer Sicilians, those who never succeeded in climbing upon the backs of their peers to middle-class affluence, have never changed a life style that goes back a thousand years; each man fathers as many sons as possible, works to support them until they are old enough to support him, and then settles back into the warm security afforded by filial devotion and responsibility.

The Chinese are scattered, their shack town long since burned down, probably as a result of a guttering lamp knocked over by some Chinese deep in another plane of consciousness, his smoldering opium pipe beside him. This story is as good as any, although some old hands hint that more likely some self-appointed civic renovator, looking upon the sleazy row of shacks along the water as a festering Oriental sore on the flank of New Monterey, moved upon it one night bearing kerosene and torches. At any rate, it was as spectacular a fire as any that blazed from time to time among the empty canneries years later.

For more than fifty years the venerable old buildings sat there, each year looking more tattered and disheveled. Through the years the continued wash of the tides, the weathering action of salt air, the corrosive action of spilled liquids from the canneries, and rust all worked to create a soft patina on wood and a rough encrustation on exposed metal. Raw timber turned warm gray, the color of the granitic rocks on which the canneries stand; iron pilings accumulated deep crusts of red, overlaid with barnacles and limpets where the waves washed against them, until their original appearance was altered beyond recall.

From the ocean side, the canneries grew to look like ancient battlements against which the sea had moved its siege troops in a constant war of attrition. Thousands of gulls, drawn by spilled fish, wheeled about, perching on pilings and roof ridges to add their own not inconsiderable patina. Beneath the outer pilings, where waves spent them-

Through half a century tides, salt air, rust, and the canneries' own corrosive liquids have worked to create a soft patina on timbers and a rough red crust on exposed metal.

selves on smooth sand, small sanderlings in search of minute crustaceans advanced and retreated before each wave in swift and perfect unison.

Then, one by one, the canneries began to burn, always in the dark of night, lighting up the whole bay so that people in Santa Cruz and Moss Landing and on the mountains above San Jose were convinced that all Monterey was ablaze. Over a period of fifteen years more than half the canneries went up in smoke. Monterey people speculated openly whether it was arson by some neurotic or arson for insurance.

The Row, that portion not gone up in smoke and flame, has suffered indignities that would have saddened Steinbeck were he to walk there now looking for the Bear Flag or Wing Chong's Emporium or La Ida's or the Pacific Biological Laboratory. Gone, all gone. La Ida's is a restaurant, Wing Chong's an antique junk shop, the Lab a self-conscious private club for mildly roistering and aging professional men, the Bear Flag—that paragon among fancy houses, whose image will surely remain peerless for all time—the Bear Flag now an empty lot beside an auto body works.

Some of the canneries, sagging, their broken windows sightless or boarded against intruders, huddle together at the east end of the street. On the west end, the others are tricked out as expensive restaurants or chic bazaars.

The street is attuned to a different rhythm now than when the whistles blasted in early mornings of the past. Now Cannery Row—no longer Ocean View Avenue but renamed officially Cannery Row by a city council that recognized when it had a good thing—comes alive when the first of an endless number of California Parlour Car Tour buses rounds the hill from Monterey, passes the Coast Guard station and the jetty, and turns into the deserted east end of the street. The bus makes a jog at the railroad track and turns into the

western end. The people in the bus, who may never have heard of Steinbeck but who joyfully recognize a tourist trap when they see one, come alert when the bus pulls up beside the old cannery in the very center of activity on the new Row. The building stands there with its weathered facade converted into a gleaming expanse of plate glass windows, behind which stands a moth-eaten old lion. Both the lion and the cannery have a certain crestfallen look about them, as if embarrassed to be caught in such an undignified condition. The tour groups never notice.

The pulse quickens, and the peak is reached when the sun goes down, the lights come up, and shining cars come streaming in to clog the streets. Their passengers fill the eating places, which look like upper-class English restaurants, Polynesian tiki huts, or hangouts of seedy Chicago hoods.

Steinbeck saddened? No, he would have cursed it fervently with mighty, unprintable oaths, turned his back upon it forever, and climbed the steep hills to share a stolen jug of wine with Danny and Pilon and Jesus Maria Corcoran, the paisanos of his fertile brain, to drink away the ugly memory in that lovely and peaceable place that existed in his mind's eye, Tortilla Flat. And when the fog came through the pines and dawn broke in a gray, dripping world, once more the boats in the bay would whistle and the canneries would answer in a mighty chorus of welcome.

The canning machines—wrapped in steam and fed by an endless supply of lids—thumped out can by can the pulse of Cannery Row.

From the fishing boats the endless silver stream poured into giant hoppers, then on conveyor belts to the cutting tables, canning machines, and shipping cartons, to be hauled away to a million waiting tables.

THE CAST OF CANNERY ROW

"*Across the street in the lot between the whorehouse and
Wing Chong's grocery, there were a number of rusty pipes, a
boiler or two, and some great timbers, all thrown there by the
canneries. A number of the free company of Cannery Row slept in
the big pipes, and when the sun was warm they would come out to
sit like lizards on the timbers. There they held social commerce.
They borrowed dimes back and forth, shared tobacco, and if
anyone brought a pint of liquor into sight, it meant that he not
only wanted to share it but intended to. They were a fairly ragged
set of men, their clothing of blue denim almost white at the knees
and buttocks from pure erosion. They were, as Ed said, the
Lotus Eaters of our era, successful in their resistance against the
nervousness and angers and frustrations of our time.*"

— The Log from the Sea of Cortez

*Along the Row there is still a welcome for
the fraternity of the footloose, the brotherhood of
the besotted.*

When people flocked to Monterey to work in the new canning industry, they were followed by those who always rush to find a need and fill it, and to turn a quick profit while about it—the sharp operators, the booze sellers, the gamblers, the pimps and whores and madams. And after these elite come the assorted human flotsam cast up on such shores—the bums, the drunks, the drifters, those who never found security and some who never sought it. For there were some among them who were remarkably successful in living a reasonably full life free of the aims and strains and disappointments of their fellow citizens dedicated to a more conventional existence.

Perhaps the combination of place and climate was such that a happy breed became the inevitable result. In all but a few weeks of the year, a man can live on these shores protected by no more than the most modest roof. And when the canneries ran full blast, it was easy to hustle the unwary for a meal, or a drink, or both. What more could a man want or need?

So it was that as Cannery Row grew, this demimonde grew apace. The street, drab and humdrum with the business of fish processing by day, came alive at dusk when the bordellos scattered along its length became magnets for all the footloose males for miles around.

If the truth were known, many of the leaders of the community and guardians of the public morals were inordinately fond of these social facilities. Consider, for instance, the time during the thirties when the editor of the *Monterey Trader*, a weekly newspaper, published an article on the fast houses operating at the time. To cap the article, he listed the license numbers of all the automobiles parked one particular noon in front of Flora Wood's establishment. The repercussions were immediate as the community gleefully discovered that most of the city officers, a contingent from the courthouse in Salinas, and a sizable number of businessmen from that very religious community Pacific Grove were spending a not inconsiderable portion of their time at Flora's. Even two millionaires from the East vacationing at the Del Monte Hotel were turned up in the general tumult.

When Steinbeck arrived upon the scene as a young man, the prototypes of many of his characters had been there for years. Ed Ricketts of the Pacific Biological Lab; Wing Chong, the Chinese storekeeper; Flora Wood, the madam; Andre Moreau, the nonobjective painter; and a host of others—all were there to walk through his pages as Doc, Lee Chong, Dora Flood, and Henri, the painter and perpetual boat builder. Those who weren't there were manufactured out of the raw material of Steinbeck's agile imagination. But even if he had never been there to record it, Cannery Row would still have been a place of warmth, gentle humor, sorrow, pathos, and human empathy on a scale almost larger than life. For the people of the streets and alleys and vacant lots of Cannery Row lived lives of far more zest than the workaday people who came to the Row, labored, and left when the work was done.

What the world looks on as eccentricity was considered normal on the Row. Look closely at Andre Moreau, he of the strange palette, wild canvases, and many women, who lived in a former two-story chicken house on the ridge above the Row, so arranged that the only entrance was through a window in the second floor, accessible only by a ladder lowered from inside the house. Not one of his neighbors thought this particularly strange; the need of a man to be left alone was understood and respected. The fact that Andre would come down to visit his friends leading his pet goat by a rope was not considered unusual either, except perhaps among the more firmly settled who sometimes demurred at entertaining the goat in their houses.

Such a community must, perforce, exert a fey influence on the more moderate world of respectable townspeople that surrounds it. Recall, if you will, the esteemed lady official of one of the towns who departed this life after having expressed a wish to be buried at sea. Her friends decided to make it an occasion to be remembered and rented the largest purse seiner in the fleet as a funeral barge. The corpse, duly enshrouded in a canvas bag, was escorted on board by a considerable number of her fellow citizens. The boat put out to sea but immediately upon passing the protection of the breakwater in the harbor encountered unexpectedly heavy swells. The less hardy became desperately ill, including the officiating ecclesiastic who was miserably contemplating the open sea from an acute angle at the rail. During the rolling and tossing passage, the mourners who were still able attached to the legs of the decedent a heavy, rusty flywheel purchased from one of the canneries to serve as a weight.

When a sufficient distance from the shore had been reached to comply with the law's demands, a wide plank was laid upon the deck, and the body, weight and all, was placed upon it. The seasick divine turned from the rail and stumbled hurriedly through the rites until he reached the point where he consigned the remains to the deep. Thereupon the seagoing pallbearers lifted the plank to the rail, preparing to tilt it high and slide the body neatly over the side. At that moment a particularly large and vicious wave caught the boat and the side where the mourners were gathered soared skyward. The corpse, with the two-hundred-pound flywheel to provide momentum, immediately became a lethal projectile loosed upon the mourners, who scattered in mortal fear until the craft returned to a relatively even keel. Twice more the gallant group attempted to slide the body overboard; twice more they fled as the heavy sea hurled the juggernaut back upon them.

Finally, in desperation, they inched the remains back along the deck to the open fantail and then gently hurled the lady and her flywheel into the waiting sea. The seiner made a tight circle around the spot in a gesture of farewell and then fled for the calm of Monterey Harbor. The ill staggered weakly ashore; the hardier headed for Flora's to toss off a toast in memory of the late departed.

From such happenings were legends made, legends to be talked about through the years, even until today, whenever men of settled age come together to pause, to remember, to recall with relish and a certain sadness the days and events on the Row that with the passage of the years have assumed dimensions far beyond any they had in the beginning.

THE VIEW FROM THE TOP

" You wouldn't know, my Charley, that right down there, in that little valley, I fished for trout with your namesake, my Uncle Charley. And over there—see where I'm pointing—my mother shot a wildcat. Straight down there, forty miles away, our old family ranch was—old starvation ranch. Can you see that darker place there? Well, that's a tiny canyon with a clear and lovely stream bordered with wild azaleas and fringed with big oaks. And on one of those oaks my father burned his name with a hot iron together with the name of the girl he loved. In the long years the bark grew over the burn and covered it. And just a little while ago, a man cut that oak for firewood and his splitting wedge uncovered my father's name and the man sent it to me. In the spring, Charley, when the valley is carpeted with blue lupines like a flowery sea, there's the smell of heaven up here, the smell of heaven."

— TRAVELS WITH CHARLEY

The oak forest of the northern Gabilans turns to subtle rust when October frosts brush the hillsides.

Fremont Peak, once called Pico de los Gavilanes by the Spaniards and Mexicans (who did not take to putting their own names on every natural feature of the land), rises up at the northern end of the Gabilans where the range almost joins the Santa Cruz Mountains to complete the encirclement of Monterey Bay and the Salinas Valley. It isn't a big mountain, as mountains go in the West, but it is respectable enough to dominate the flat valley near where it meets the sea.

The road to the top begins in San Juan Bautista, where the hills surrounding the town rise up gently to the crest of the mountain and the peak itself resembles nothing so much as a sharp point on a longer ridge. The road goes past limestone caves near the bottom of the mountain and makes its way gracefully up out of green pepper fields into canyons whose sides are covered with oak and buckeye; the scarlet of poison oak is everywhere. The road goes on past small horse ranches, up to where the homes of pensioners are nestled in clearings hacked out of the brush.

It passes the Mormon church, sitting neat and tidy like some well-kept colonial church of New England. The road, narrowing, begins to climb shortly until it rises above the woodlands and reaches the chamise- and manzanita-covered slopes. Off to the northeast is the town of Hollister. Between there and San Juan Bautista, spread out in the valley, are the brilliant patchworks of the Ferry-Morse flower seed farm.

The road eventually reaches a higher forest area, this time of big-cone pine and California black oak, its leaves golden in the autumn light. In the late afternoon the woods are aflame with gold and crimson. Quail scuttle through the dry grass, blue plumes jerking and bobbing. Deer graze calmly among trees alive with migrating birds.

Where the road ends, a path goes on up the peak to where the Channel 8 transmitter sits, a tower festooned with red blinking lights, microwave reflectors, and all the other mysterious attachments common to such monuments.

A little farther on and higher yet is the rocky pinnacle where Frémont is said to have planted the American flag in a defiant gesture toward the assembled Mexican soldiery below. This is the very top of the Gabilans and a good place to sit and look about and think great thoughts—or not to think at all. It is quiet here, only a faint breeze from the ocean twenty miles away ruffling the low brown grasses and an occasional descending arpeggio of a canyon wren breaking the silence.

Off in the northwest stands tall Loma Prieta, highest of the Santa Cruz Mountains. East of it, across the Santa Clara Valley, are the white domes of the observatories on Mount Hamilton, above San Jose. Smoke and haze from the cities gathered around San Francisco Bay float southward along the same route as Highway 101, down through Coyote and Morgan Hill and Gilroy, over the low Aromas hills, and into the broad plain of the Salinas basin. The low afternoon sun turns the haze to white gold.

In the southwest, rising steeply above the haze, the high ridges of the Santa Lucias rise up behind Mount Toro, rank upon rank, and march off into the distance toward Paso Robles, a hundred miles south. From this distance their rugged slopes have a soft, blue, velvety look.

Below, spread out like a huge horn of plenty (which it is indeed), the Salinas Valley stretches from the sea to where it disappears into the blue haze far to the southeast. Its fields are laid out in little patches like some huge, colored crossword puzzle. Here and there the sun glitters on a pond or flashes momentarily from windshields of automobiles hurtling down the freeway.

Elkhorn Slough, vestigial remnant of the mighty Sacramento when it flowed this way before the Golden Gate was ever formed, shines out brightly, a long scimitar of silver in the west.

The yellow glow on the mountains begins to turn to orange as the sun sinks into the veil of dust and smoke that mantles the earth. The slopes of Fremont Peak, receding into the valley below, begin to take on a tawny hue. Almost as high as the pinnacle itself, a red-tailed hawk rides the currents of the western slope. The rays of the sun strike its copper feathers, and the bird bursts into flame on the wing.

The mountain grows quieter as the evening breezes subside. There is a feeling of eternalness here. But where the western slope meets the valley below, the steam shovels of a magnesium manufacturer have removed large chunks of the mountain to extract its dolomite; on the eastern shoulder of the peak a cement company has taken away most of a smaller ridge to get at its limestone. So these mountains are not impregnable, not eternal. They change, as the valley does. Whether the change is for better or worse must be judged by future generations.

Several generations of the present and the past have left their mark on the valley below, inscribing it with a sometimes heavy and callous hand. But Nature can be compassionate—the sun sinking to the horizon beyond the Monterey headland turns the valley between the ranges into lavender and the hills to palest gold. Suddenly there is a great emptiness, a violet, soundless void broken only by scattered specks of light in Salinas and Gonzales and Chualar and Watsonville and the farmhouses clustered along the roads.

For a long, lingering moment of time, a ghostly procession comes out of the darkness of the valley —naked Indians pursued by the saintly Serra, Spanish soldiers in ragged leather and tarnished armor, Mexican vaqueros at a gallop, dust exploding beneath the hooves of their lathered horses. There are Yankee ships and Chinese junks and covered wagons, tattered and creaking and spent. There are hordes of Portuguese and Sicilians and haggard Okies in their steaming jalopies.

And bringing up the rear, like some raucous calliope at the end of this human circus, comes a rattling, jolting wayward bus. Hanging from its windows are a noisy, motley crew of saints and sons-of-bitches: Doc and Mac and Gay and Pilon and Portagee Joe, the Pirate with all his dogs and Wide Ida with all her girls, and Suzy and Hazel and the Widow Morales, and in the driver's seat, behind the cracked and dusty windshield, that bearded, grizzled, tale-spinning son of this valley and these shores, John Steinbeck.

From Gabilan Peak—where Frémont's arrogant company once snarled defiance at the Mexicans— Steinbeck Country stretches quietly away to the sea.

AFTERWORD

I first saw the long Salinas Valley from the windows of one of the Southern Pacific's finest trains while traveling as a vassal of the United States Army. During two tours of duty at Fort Ord, a love affair began with the hills and forests of the Monterey Peninsula, the cliffs and summits of the Big Sur, and the lovely valleys of the Salinas and the Carmel—a love affair that has flourished, grown stronger and more fervent during twenty-five years of living here.

Over the years it has been an unending joy to explore the length and breadth of Monterey County and to photograph it in all its moods and seasons. But not until a friend took me up to fly over the Salinas Valley in his airplane did there become a different dimension to the land. These new viewpoints resulted in new and different images, and planted the thought of a photographic essay on Monterey County—an idea that expanded and grew, took shape and new directions, and eventually became this book.

From the very beginning it was important to me that the book be primarily a visual experience, and therefore it became a book not about Steinbeck but rather about Steinbeck Country—the land in which he grew up, which must have formed him and stimulated him in much the same way that it stimulated me. But where Steinbeck concerned himself mainly with the people of this land and turned his thoughts and his pen to them, my interest lies in the land itself in all its forms and manifestations.

These then are the pictures and the words that reflect a love affair with a land that I have grown to cherish above all others.

It may be that once there was a book that came into being entirely through the efforts of its author, but it is doubtful that this is so. Certainly this one was assisted along its way by many friends who aided in one way or another.

First there was Jim Forkner, who took me up in his Cessna and showed me a new world below; then Ann Sumida Tsuchiya and Kay Hilliard, who provided the first impetus; Buck Wiley, who opened innumerable doors and vistas for me; and Roy Bray, Robert Marble, and Julius Trescony, who allowed me to wander freely about their great ranches.

I am indebted to Jimmie Costello and Ted Durein of the *Monterey Peninsula Herald;* to Beth Ingals and Harrydick Ross for sharing their memories of Steinbeck Country; to Winston Elstob for his knowledge concerning the long-vanished Chinese and for his introductions into the migrant Mexican communities of the Salinas Valley; to Jack Swanson for his aid and knowledge concerning cattle ranching; to Fred Crummey for his help in the Corral de Tierra; to Sally Calabrese and Sal Ferrante for assistance in photographing the fishing fleet; to Tom Alioti for aid in procuring access to the last remaining cannery; and to David Walton for his untiring aid in providing local color.

Thanks are due to Sheila Baldridge of the Harrison Memorial Library in Carmel for her assistance in historical research, and to Barbara Sims for her help in the early stages of the manuscript. I am in the debt of Ansel Adams, Joan Daniels Manley, Ernest Braun, Leland Lewis, David Cavagnaro, and William Brandon for sharing their knowledge in the field of book publishing, and to the editors of the *Monterey Peninsula Herald* for permission to include the segment on Pon Chung, originally written as an article for the *Herald* a number of years ago.

I am most grateful to my wife who was a constant source of encouragement. Finally, I am indebted to all the others who helped but whom I have possibly overlooked in this brief passage; without their aid, this book would not have been possible.

PHOTOGRAPHIC NOTES

All of the photographs in this book were made with cameras using either 4x5 film or 120 roll film. The great majority were made with a single lens reflex, the Mamiya RB 67, which has an overall format of $2\frac{1}{4}"x2\frac{3}{4}"$. I have two lenses for it, a 90mm and a 250mm. In addition a few were made with the Mamiyaflex C2 with a 180mm lens. The aerial photographs were made with a Rolleiflex with an 80mm lens.

The 4x5 camera is a Calumet view camera; its lenses are a 65mm Super Angulon, a 90mm Super Angulon, a 135mm Schneider Xenar, a $6\frac{3}{8}"$ Wollensak Raptar, an 8″ Schneider Symmar, a 10″ Schneider Tele-Arton, and a 14″ Commercial Ektar.

In working with any camera, I prefer to make every photograph from a tripod. Sometimes with the smaller cameras, however, this was not possible, and the quality of the image suffered.

In monochrome, I use Ansco Versapan sheet film and Panatomic-X and Tri-X roll film. Ansel Adams's Zone System for exposure and development was followed; prints were made on Ilfobrom doubleweight paper, developed in Amidol.

Some of the older color photographs were made on 4x5 Anscochrome and Agfachrome. Most, however, were made on Ektachrome which has a speed of 50 in both sheet and roll film. I use this film not because it is better—both Anscochrome and Agfachrome are excellent films—but because it is more readily available, and there are many processing laboratories for it.

I keep no notes on exposures of color films since I expose color with a Norwood meter, and it rarely leads me astray. I keep notes on the black-and-white exposures only to determine the development time in the darkroom. Once the print is made, notes are of no further use and are discarded. Information concerning lens setting and shutter speed mean nothing unless a dozen or more variables are taken into consideration.

In the photographic notes below, camera and lens are indicated. Since most of the photographs were made with Ektachrome professional film, no mention is made unless some other film was used.

I would emphasize that the mechanical equipment used to make any photograph is the least important link in the chain of events that is photography; the pieces of crucial equipment are the eye behind the camera and the brain that evaluates what the eye sees and then says yes or no.

Photographic details

PAGES 2–3: Dawn over the Salinas Valley, from Cone Peak in the Santa Lucias. Calumet, 14″ Ektar, Agfachrome.

PAGES 4–5: Moss on valley oaks, Carmel-Greenfield Road in the Santa Lucias. Calumet, 14″ Ektar.

PAGES 6–7: Reflections in Monterey Harbor. Mamiya, 90mm Sekor.

PAGES 8–9: Grainfield on the Wiley Ranch near Soledad. Mamiya, 90mm Sekor.

PAGES 12–13: Fog over Point Lobos. Mamiya, 90mm Sekor.

PAGE 14: Surf below Bixby Creek bridge, Big Sur. Mamiya, 250mm Sekor.

PAGE 18: The Santa Lucias near Arroyo Seco. Mamiya, 250mm Sekor.

PAGE 20: Sunrise on Plaskett Ridge, Big Sur. Calumet, 8″ Symmar, Agfachrome.

PAGE 23: Rock cliffs, Machete Ridge, the Pinnacles National Monument. Calumet, 8″ Symmar, Agfachrome.

PAGE 24: Chamise on high ridges of the Pinnacles. Mamiya, 90mm Sekor.

PAGE 25: Lichen, the Pinnacles. Mamiya, 90mm Sekor.

PAGE 27: Peeling bark of madrone tree (*Arbutus menziesii*) near Chews Ridge, Santa Lucia Range. Calumet, $6\frac{3}{8}"$ Raptar, Anscochrome.

PAGE 29; TOP: Deer in grainfield, near Slacks Canyon in the Gabilans. Mamiya, 250mm Sekor. BOTTOM: Potrero on Rana Creek Ranch, Sierra de Salinas, Santa Lucia Range. Mamiyaflex C2, 180mm Sekor.

PAGES 30–31: Sunset in the Santa Lucias from Post Road, Big Sur. Calumet, 8″ Symmar, Agfachrome.

PAGES 32-33: Storm clouds during autumn equinox from coastal ridge above Pacific Valley in Big Sur. Calumet, 8″ Symmar, Kodak Infrared, No. 29 red filter.

PAGE 34: Aerial, ranch roads in the hills east of King City. Rolleiflex, Panatomic-X, G filter.

PAGE 35: Aerial, lower slopes of the Santa Lucias near Soledad. Rolleiflex, Panatomic-X, G filter.

PAGE 36: Field on Lonoak Road east of King City. Calumet, 14″ Ektar, Ansco Versapan.

PAGE 37: Aerial, plastic-covered strawberry fields near Soledad. Rolleiflex, Panatomic-X, G filter.

PAGE 38: Aerial, plowed fields and farm roads near Soledad. Rolleiflex, Panatomic-X, G filter.

PAGE 39: Lonoak Road east of King City. Calumet, 14″ Ektar, Ansco Versapan.

PAGE 40: Hills and fields, Bitterwater Valley, east of King City. Calumet, 14″ Ektar, Ansco Versapan, A filter.

PAGE 41: Clearing fog, Big Sur hills on Rancho El Sur. Calumet, 8″ Symmar, Ansco Versapan.

PAGES 42-43: Surf near Carmel. Mamiyaflex C2, 180mm Sekor, Panatomic-X, G filter.

PAGE 44: Corral de Tierra from Mount Toro, with ocean fogs over Monterey in distance. Calumet, 8″ Symmar, Ansco Versapan, A filter.

PAGE 47: Old barn door, Corral de Tierra. Calumet, 8″ Symmar, Ansco Versapan.

PAGE 49; TOP: Baby blue-eyes (*Nemophila menziesii*), Corral de Tierra. Mamiyaflex C2, 180mm Sekor. BOTTOM: Sunset fogs, Sierra de Salinas. Mamiyaflex C2, 180mm Sekor.

PAGE 50: Spring in the Sierra de Salinas above Corral de Tierra. Calumet, 14″ Ektar, Agfachrome.

PAGE 51: Abandoned schoolhouse, Corral de Tierra. Mamiya, 90mm Sekor.

PAGE 52: Salinas River near Chualar. Mamiya, 90mm Sekor, polarizing filter.

PAGE 55; TOP: Strawberry fields with plastic covers, Arroyo Seco Road near Soledad. Mamiyaflex C2, 180mm Sekor. BOTTOM: Irrigated sugar beet field, near Chualar. Mamiya, 90mm Sekor.

PAGE 56: Overhead irrigation, Wiley Ranch near Soledad. Calumet, 14″ Ektar.

PAGE 57: Water plants, Salinas River near its mouth. Mamiya, 90mm Sekor.

PAGES 58-59: Salinas River at dusk from old bridge at San Lucas. Mamiya, 90mm Sekor.

PAGE 62: Monterey cypress (*Cupressus macrocarpa*) on cliffs of Seventeen Mile Drive. B&J Press, 6⅜″ Raptar, Anscochrome.

PAGE 64; TOP: Gull on rock, Carmel Bay. Mamiyaflex C2, 180mm Sekor. BOTTOM: South shore, Point Lobos. Calumet, 90mm Super Angulon, polarizing filter.

PAGE 65: Sunset at Carmel. Calumet, 14″ Ektar, Agfachrome.

PAGES 66-67: North shore, Point Lobos. Calumet, 8″ Symmar.

PAGE 68; TOP: Mussels and starfish on granite rocks, Pacific Grove. Mamiya, 90mm Sekor. BOTTOM: Wrack at Point Pinos. Rolleiflex, 80mm Xenar.

PAGE 69; TOP: Starfish on rocks along Cannery Row. Mamiya, 90mm Sekor. BOTTOM: Detail of abalone shell. Calumet, 90mm Super Angulon, Anscochrome. The bellows was greatly extended so that long exposure was necessary with corrections in exposure for reciprocity failure.

PAGES 70-71: Monterey Peninsula from hills above Corral de Tierra. Calumet, 14″ Ektar. This photograph was a double exposure. At twilight an exposure was made at one stop less than that indicated by the meter to register landforms and some detail but to avoid too much sky exposure. After complete darkness a second exposure was made to register the lights of the city. Since both exposures were made at f22, the second exposure required a time of five minutes.

PAGE 72; TOP: Sunset, Carmel Bay. Mamiyaflex C2, 180mm Sekor, 10R filter. BOTTOM: Bird tracks at sunset, Pacific Grove. Mamiya, 90mm Sekor.

PAGE 75: Fog in pine forest, Riley Ranch near Point Lobos. Mamiyaflex C2, 180mm Sekor.

PAGE 76-77: Winter in Robinson Canyon, Santa Lucia Range. Calumet, 8″ Symmar. Blue of the photograph is because entire light source in this shaded canyon was from bright blue sky above. No corrective filter was available at the moment.

PAGE 78: Big Sur Coast below Nepenthe. Mamiya, 90mm Sekor, Polarizing filter.

PAGES 80-81: Sunset, Little Sur rivermouth, Big Sur. Calumet, 14″ Ektar.

PAGES 82-83: After sunset, Sand Dollar Beach in Big Sur. Calumet, 14″ Ektar.

PAGE 86: Late afternoon, Big Sur coast. Mamiya, 90mm Sekor.

PAGE 87: Afternoon, Big Sur coast below Nacimiento Grade. Calumet, 14″ Ektar, Agfachrome.

PAGES 88-89: Farms near San Juan Bautista. Calumet, 14″ Ektar, polarizing filter.

PAGE 90: Poppies (*Eschscholzia californica*) and lupines (*Lupinus nanus*), Santa Lucia Range. Hasselblad, 80mm Planar.

PAGE 91: New leaves, California black oak (*Quercus kelloggii*), Anderson Peak, Santa Lucia Range. Mamiya, 90mm Sekor.

PAGE 92: Budding branches of a buckeye tree (*Aesculus californica*), the Pinnacles. Calumet, 8″ Symmar.

PAGE 93: Lupine (*Lupinus succulentus*) after rain, Salinas Valley. Calumet, 8″ Symmar.

PAGE 94; TOP: Fuchsia-flowered gooseberry (*Ribes speciosum*), Rana Creek Ranch, Carmel Valley. Mamiyaflex C2, 180mm Sekor. BOTTOM: Wallflower (*Erysium capitatum*), Marble Peak, Santa Lucia Range. Mamiya, 90mm Sekor.

PAGE 95; TOP: Weed, Santa Lucia Range. Mamiya, 250mm Sekor. BOTTOM LEFT: Double-exposure of brodiaea and grass in Carmel Valley—an accident that succeeded. Mamiyaflex C2, 180mm Sekor. BOTTOM RIGHT: Grass, the Pinnacles. Mamiyaflex C2, 180mm Sekor.

PAGE 96: Windmill on the Mee Ranch, Gabilan Range east of San Lucas. Mamiya, 90mm Sekor, polarizing filter.

PAGE 98: Poison oak (*Rhus diversiloba*) and madrone (*Arbutus menziesii*), Los Burros district, Santa Lucia Range. Calumet, 90mm Super Angulon.

PAGE 99; LEFT: Autumn in grape vineyard, Salinas Valley. Mamiyaflex C2, 180mm Sekor. RIGHT: Frost, Rana Creek Ranch, Carmel Valley. Mamiya, 90mm Sekor.

PAGES 102-103: Afternoon fog advancing up Salinas Valley near Greenfield. Mamiya, 90mm Sekor.

Page 106: Sunrise over fog-filled Salinas Valley. Mamiya, 90mm Sekor.

Pages 110-111: Fog, Santa Lucia Range south of Nacimiento Grade, Big Sur. Calumet, 14″ Ektar, Agfachrome.

PAGES 112-113: Joe Balestreri, skipper of the *Tage,* Monterey. Mamiya, 90mm Sekor, Tri-X, in open shade. In the interests of book design, this photograph was reversed.

PAGE 114: Intersection, Salinas Valley. Mamiya, 250mm Sekor, Panatomic-X, A filter. This is the only photograph made to meet the demands of book layout and design.

PAGE 120: Juan Arellana and daughter, labor camp, Salinas Valley. Mamiya, 250mm Sekor, Panatomic-X.

PAGE 125: Sixto Torres, labor camp, Salinas Valley. Mamiya, 250mm Sekor, Tri-X.

PAGE 126: Carlos Landero in sugarbeet field, Salinas Valley. Mamiya, 90mm Sekor, Panatomic-X, G filter.

Page 127: Celery planting in the Salinas Valley. Mamiya, 90mm Sekor, Plus-X.

PAGE 128: Roy Bray, rancher of the Lonoak. Mamiya, 90mm Sekor, Plus-X.

PAGE 131: Buck Wiley, Salinas Valley farmer. Mamiya, 90mm Sekor, Panatomic-X.

PAGE 133: Fred Tuttle on the Rancho San Lucas, Salinas Valley. Mamiya, 250mm Sekor, Panatomic-X.

PAGE 137; TOP: Apricot picker, Wiley Ranch, Soledad. Mamiyaflex C2, 180mm Sekor. BOTTOM: Garlic harvest, Wiley Ranch. Mamiya, 90mm Sekor.

PAGES 138-139: Field crews thinning celery, Salinas Valley. Mamiya, 90mm Sekor.

PAGES 140-141: Bean thrasher, Salinas Valley near Gonzales. Mamiya, 250mm Sekor.

PAGE 141: Lima bean harvesters near Greenfield. Mamiya, 90mm Sekor.

PAGES 142-143: Cattle, Rana Creek Ranch, Carmel Valley. Mamiya, 90mm Sekor.

PAGE 144: Old header wagon, Rancho San Lucas. Mamiya, 90mm Sekor, polarizing filter.

PAGE 145; TOP: Saddle, Rancho San Lucas. BOTTOM: Spurs, Rancho San Lucas. Both Mamiya, 90mm Sekor.

PAGES 146-147: Ranch buildings near San Lucas. Calumet, 8″ Symmar.

PAGE 148: Jack Swanson, horsebreaker, Cachagua Valley, Santa Lucia Range. Mamiya, 90mm Sekor.

PAGE 149; TOP: Cowboy roping horse, Cachagua Valley. Mamiya, 90mm Sekor. BOTTOM: Winter branding, Rana Creek Ranch, Carmel Valley. Mamiya, 250mm Sekor.

PAGE 150: Pon Chung. Mamiya, 90mm Sekor.

PAGES 156-157: Wake of fishing boat off Point Sur. Mamiya, 90mm Sekor.

PAGE 158: The catch on the *El Salvatore*. Mamiya, 90mm Sekor.

PAGE 161; TOP: Unloading the catch, Monterey wharf. Mamiya, 90mm Sekor. BOTTOM: Fishermen and their catch of rock cod, which they call *boccaccio,* or "big mouth" for obvious reasons. Mamiya, 90mm Sekor.

PAGES 162-163: Pulling in the net on the *El Salvatore* off Point Sur. Mamiya, 90mm Sekor.

PAGE 164: Abandoned cannery in fog at sunset. Mamiya, 90mm Sekor.

PAGE 167: Cannery Row. Mamiya, 90mm Sekor.

PAGE 170: Rusty pipes and wreckage, both on Cannery Row. Mamiya, 90mm Sekor.

PAGE 171: Surf around pilings beneath an old cannery. Mamiya, 90mm Sekor.

PAGE 173: Canning machine, Hovden Cannery. Mamiya, 90mm Sekor.

PAGE 174; TOP: Tin cans pouring down chute in cannery. Mamiyaflex C2, 180mm Sekor. Slow shutter speed used so that motion of cans would not be frozen. BOTTOM: Steam from leaking pipes in cannery. Mamiyaflex C2, 180mm Sekor. In all interior photographs in cannery, tungsten light on daylight film imparted a warm color.

PAGE 175; TOP: Packing squid in cans, Hovden Cannery. BOTTOM: Women at the packing tables, Hovden Cannery. Both photographs Mamiya, 90mm Sekor.

PAGE 176: Bum, Cannery Row. Mamiya, 90mm Sekor. This photograph necessitated an exposure of approximately 30 seconds in order that ambient light could slightly outline the buildings and the man's body. Light from the flaring match was of about 5 seconds duration.

PAGE 177: "Wino" on Cannery Row. Mamiya, 90mm Sekor.

PAGES 180-181: Autumn foliage on the slopes of Fremont Peak, Gabilan Range. Calumet, 8″ Symmar.

PAGES 184-185: Sun filtering through haze and drifting fog on Fremont Peak. Calumet, 8″ Symmar, Anscochrome.

INDEX

Body type, 11-point Bembo; display faces, Centaur and Rivoli. Composition by Paul O. Giesey/Adcrafters, Portland, Oregon.

Design by Dannelle Lazarus.